# The Gift

a spiritual autobiography

Anna Jeffery

The Gift

Copyright © Anna Jeffery 2017 All Rights Reserved
The rights of Anna Jeffery to be identified as the author of this work have been asserted in accordance with the Copyright, Designs and Patents Act 1988
All rights reserved. No part may be reproduced, adapted, stored in a retrieval system or transmitted by any means, electronic, mechanical, photocopying, or otherwise without the prior written permission of the author or publisher.

Spiderwize
Remus House
Coltsfoot Drive
Woodston
Peterborough
PE2 9BF

www.spiderwize.com

A CIP catalogue record for this book is available from the British Library.

The views expressed in this work are solely those of the author and do not necessarily reflect the views of the publisher, and the publisher hereby disclaims any responsibility for them.

ISBN: 978-1-911113-92-8

*For Michael, Judy & Bobbin
all of whom encouraged me to share
this faith journey*

*Our spiritual journey connects us to the source of that indwelling happiness and wholeness – the great mystery we so often refer to as God – the invisible, ineffable presence that is the source of all life. There is a gift in every experience, no matter how difficult or painful.*

*Source Unknown*

# AUTHOR'S INTRODUCTION

In this new work, I have taken as my theme Blake's immortal words:

*I give you the end of a golden string:*
*Only wind it into a ball,*
*It will lead you in at Heaven's Gate*
*Built in Jerusalem's wall.*

*William Blake*
*Epigrams, Verses and Fragments for the Note Book*

For most of my adult life, an awareness of the spiritual dimension has served as an ongoing strength – a Gift – offered to each one of us but, as with all gifts, it requires the response of acceptance or rejection. Because of my conviction, I have been inspired to help those preoccupied with material wealth and values to seek a more meaningful approach to life by accepting the Gift. My own faith journey is the factor underpinning each of my five spiritual projects and the conviction that the value of spirituality is priceless has proved to be the greatest strength in my life.

And so by holding tightly to the golden string (of faith) readers can embark on their own journey of exploration and thus discover the immeasurable value of the spiritual dimension in their lives.

Blake's image postulates that the end of this golden string (of faith) is there for each of us to find but rather than merely following it, we should actively wind it into a ball – if we don't keep the string taut and keep winding, we may lose our way and wander into unknown territory, but by winding and following in faith, it will surely lead us to our rightful destination of which Blake writes so eloquently – Heaven's Gate.

'The Gift' is not only an account of my own faith journey, it shows how you too can transform your life, just by taking hold of that golden string!

**AJ**
**Summer 2016**

# ABOUT THE AUTHOR

Anna Jeffery lives in Surrey with her architect husband Michael. She has a background of health service, school and church administration combined with a deeply held Christian faith; for many years she has been aware of an inner drive to help others come to that same shared faith.

She has an identical twin sister and the account of their inter-twined lives features prominently in 'The Gift'.

In 1992 she launched Cultural Country Retreats, a national network of retreats 'with a difference' primarily for those on the fringe of the church who were seeking a meaningful spiritual dimension to their lives. These were held at some of the finest retreat houses in the UK, providing a cultural and rural framework within which spiritual thought and reflection could take place. The blend of rural setting, musical input (classical music festivals) and buildings of rich historical interest, together with spiritual themes, enriched the lives of all who participated. The retreats which ran for many years, are currently being restructured.

Now retired, Anna is currently running the fifth of her five spiritual projects – Words, Music, Stillness – a discussion group based on the five books in the Vision series, edited by Rev. William Sykes, former chaplain of University College, Oxford. She writes regularly for New Vision, the journal of the Hamblin Trust. She also works in a voluntary capacity with local charities. And takes time just To Be!

'The Gift' is Anna's third book. Her first, 'Five Gold Rings', was published by Darton, Longman and Todd in 2003; her second, 'Symphony of Life', was published by Diadem Books in 2009.

\* \* \*

# FOREWORD

Here is another fine work from the pen of Anna Jeffery – her best yet. Looking at life with the eyes of faith, she explores and demonstrates the presence and activity of God in who she is and what she has done.

In an unusual and inspiring autobiography, she focuses on the major events of her life; the ventures she has initiated, the people who have inspired and empowered her; the places she loves and which speak to her so powerfully; and random events which have come her way revealing the coherent and loving working of the Spirit, weaving that 'golden thread' through her life.

This is a positive and inspiring piece of writing which should encourage anyone who is searching for life's meaning, to read it and be reassured that spirituality is indeed a reality rather than a myth. It comes from a deep personal faith in a Loving God who is at work in the life of everyone He has created.

I strongly recommend this book. Readers will not be disappointed.


John Dennis
(formerly Bishop of St. Edmundsbury and Ipswich)
Winchester, September 2016

# CONTENTS

About The Author .................................................................................vii
Foreword ................................................................................................ix

## SECTION I
I     Early Years ................................................................................2
II    Career Developments & Marriage ............................................4
III   Emergence of Faith ...................................................................6
IV   A Dark Time ..............................................................................7

## SECTION II
The Twinship ..................................................................................10

## SECTION III - The Spiritual Projects
I     Cultural Country Retreats.........................................................20
II    Five Gold Rings .......................................................................32
III   St. George's House Windsor Castle .......................................44
IV   Symphony of Life.....................................................................50
V    Words, Music, Stillness ...........................................................57
VI   A Cathedral Dream ..................................................................61

## SECTION IV
I     Articles Written for 'New Vision' ...........................................66
      (The Magazine of The Hamblin Trust)
II    The Heart of The Matter: A Personal Credo...........................67
III   Acceptance ...............................................................................70
IV   A Trilogy on Truth...................................................................72
V    Essential Connections .............................................................75
VI   Held In Perfect Balance...........................................................78

## SECTION V
I     St. Cuthman's Retreat House ..................................................82
II    St. Columba's Retreat House ..................................................84
III   Cathedral of The Isles, Cumbrae..............................................85
IV   Portmeirion ...............................................................................87
V    Harry Edwards Healing Sanctuary ..........................................89
VI   Orchard Cottage .......................................................................92

## SECTION VI

| | | |
|---|---|---:|
| I | Sixth Form Awakenings | 96 |
| II | Father Alan Cotgrove, Cowley Fathers | 97 |
| III | An Oxford Mystic | 98 |
| IV | Rev. Dr. Douglas Young | 99 |
| V | Rt. Rev. John Dennis | 103 |
| VI | The Very Rev. Alex Wedderspoon | 104 |
| VII | Intimations of Life After Death | 111 |
| VIII | The Fintry Community | 114 |

## SECTION VII
Highdays & Holidays .................................................................. 118

## SECTION VIII
Earning A Crust ......................................................................... 122

## SECTION IX
Rounding Off ............................................................................. 126

## SECTION X - Afterwords
Tapestry of My Life ................................................................... 131
When Earth's Last Picture Is Painted by Rudyard Kipling ............ 132
Acknowledgements ................................................................... 134

## INDEX .................................................................................. 136

*What I do is me: for that I came*
*As Kingfishers Catch Fire*

Gerard Manley Hopkins

# SECTION 1

Part I: Early Years

Part II: Career Developments & Marriage

Part III: Emergence of Faith

Part IV: A Dark Time

# I

## EARLY YEARS

My twin sister, Judy, and I were born in Hereford in the early part of the Second World War, but into a loveless marriage. Our parents, who were totally incompatible, fought each other verbally and psychologically all through our childhood and beyond. Because of this deeply unhappy environment, Judy and I became immensely close and created our own imaginary world with a variety of characters, each with their own voices and personalities. Even today when we are on our own, we occasionally revert to type and act out these fantasy figures – it's a twin thing!

And it was only as we grew older that we realised such an atmosphere of constant tension – rows and upsets – was not part of normal married life. But despite their deteriorating relationship, my sister and I were loved unconditionally by both parents and this undoubtedly contributed hugely to our development into two reasonable human beings.

However, as we grew through teens and beyond, we were increasingly aware of an impending disaster – our mother sought refuge from her deep unhappiness by resorting to alcohol and sleeping pills – a lethal mix by any standards.

Meanwhile, my father had not fallen victim to the 1918 flu pandemic but the germ lay dormant in his brain only to emerge years later as a form of encephalitis (so we were told). He subsequently developed a brain disorder, manifesting as a tormenting obsessional neurosis - a compulsion to read repeatedly all and anything he could lay his hands on. Indeed he could spend the whole of one day just reading the words on a matchbox over and over again. This eventually necessitated brain surgery in the form of a frontal leucotomy. The stress finally became too much for our mother and she left him – but the spectre of financial insecurity resulted in the ultimate humiliation of having to return to him simply for a roof over her head. By that time, my father's brain surgery had alleviated his obsession with reading but the condition subsequently re-emerged in a new form involving a complex regime of counting, based on the number nine. This new obsession re-ignited my mother's deteriorating mental health and, while in a restaurant one evening with my father, she choked to death – at the tender age of 57.

The resultant shock and sudden trauma had unimaginable effects on all of us. My father died a few years later while confined to a nursing home – tormented to the end by his obsessive neurosis. Thus both our parents suffered a desperately sad end to their lives.

Meanwhile, my sister and I had no other choice but to move on with our own lives. We moved to Reading and attended college there while sharing a flat together. Judy married soon after and remained in Reading for several years. Her marriage and the inevitable 'barrier' that the presence of her husband created within the twinship meant major adjustments for both of us – especially for me. But cataclysmic though it seemed, life does not stand still and the choice was to sink or swim; thus I started swimming for my life!

And for me, it was another 15 or more, lonely years, without the close companionship of my twin, before I met the man who would become the light of my own life and those 15 intervening years were years of challenge, adventure, setbacks, periods of happiness and deep sadness.

# II

# CAREER DEVELOPMENTS & MARRIAGE

After Reading and my sister's marriage, career changes took me to Oxford, the Radcliffe Infirmary and new friends. But life in Oxford eventually became bleak and I spread my wings further by moving to London for administrative work at The Royal College of Surgeons plus my own flat in St. John's Wood. Some years later, a chance meeting at the Marylebone Liberals, led me to the light of my life, Michael, an architect, who subsequently became my husband. His two sons from an earlier marriage, Simon and Timothy, both became an integral and key part of our lives together as did their five children – our grandchildren.

Michael is an absolute dear – 'a giant of a man' highly principled, inscrutable, enigmatic, full of his father's charm, with rugged and refined good looks characterised by that beautifully modulated deep voice that marks him from the rest. A loner, like myself, who needs his own space, as indeed do I, as counselled by Kahlil Gibran: **'stand together, but let there be spaces in your togetherness, let the wind blow between you.'** Deeply held spiritual beliefs underpin our marriage and as soul mates, with mutual respect and love, we have explored together concepts such as reincarnation, psychic studies, spirit healing, all of interest to both of us. Michael has, throughout our forty plus years together, truly been 'my rock' – supporting me 100% and giving me the freedom I needed to develop the five spiritual projects. We have both so valued the togetherness, stability and partnership a later marriage has given where compatibility in so many areas has provided a safe haven from which to meet the world and its challenges.

Michael and I married in 1975 and moved from London to Guildford where he had deep rooted family connections and I secured a post as Centre Administrator at the Guildford Postgraduate Medical Education Centre, a post I held for nearly 10 years and, being a born organiser, I loved every minute!

*Michael – in earlier days preparing for his
Everest Trek to Base Camp*

# III

## EMERGENCE OF FAITH

I soon realised that these wonderful organisational opportunities which had been gifted to me, would prove an excellent grounding in the organisation of the spiritual projects I would undertake later in life.

Other work followed where my career continued fruitfully, during which I became increasingly aware of a developing faith and a deep longing, almost a missionary zeal, to help others become aware of the value of spirituality in their own lives. Faith for me is based on an intuitive certainty that has triumphed over doubt many times over.

**Spirituality may be defined as a broad concept, bringing a sense of connection to something bigger than ourselves – bringing meaning into our lives – a universal human need. It goes beyond religious or cultural boundaries. Spirituality is characterised by faith, a search for meaning and purpose in life, a sense of connection with others and a transcendence of self, resulting in a sense of inner peace and well-being.**

# IV

# A DARK TIME

However, towards the end of 2004, after a routine mammogram, I was recalled for further tests, before the devastating revelation that I had breast cancer, not in one but both breasts and so began my cancer journey. Worse was to come as further investigations revealed the cancer had spread to my lymph nodes, requiring two bouts of surgery, chemotherapy for three months, followed by five weeks of daily radiotherapy with the subsequent trauma of hair loss, weight loss and all the other miseries associated with the treatment. I clearly recall the comments of the Consultant when I protested at the thought of months of treatment and a 'miserable Spring' as I put it. 'Yes,' he said, 'but this is to ensure you have many more Springs in the future!' A sobering thought indeed.

With cancer I found the body goes into 'self-protection' mode – a cross between anaesthesia and denial – it just doesn't seem real and one proceeds through the treatment in a kind of daze. However, ultimately one emerges from the long tunnel that is cancer. There is no doubt that a diagnosis of this magnitude brings one immediately to appreciate one's own mortality – you quickly learn not to take a single day for granted and to redefine your values and your perceived mission in life.

William Barclay puts it beautifully in his comments on The Letter to the Romans:

**We do not need to be very old to look back on life and see that things that we thought were disasters worked out to our good; things that we thought were disappointments worked out to greater blessings. We can look back and we can see a guiding and a directing hand in it and through it all.**

And through all of this, I was wonderfully supported by the medical team, friends and family and as I write, I have been in remission for 12 years.

'Lord give me health until my work is done and work until my life is done' – a prayer I have used many, many times.

And so it was that by holding tightly to the end of that golden string, I subsequently embarked on the Five Spiritual Projects (see p.20 onwards).

* * *

# SECTION II

## The Twinship

# THE TWINSHIP

Being a twin and having a twin, is a source of great joy and certainly a relationship entirely taken for granted. One simply cannot imagine life without the other.

However it is inevitable that while childhood is shared, when the time comes to move into adulthood, working life and marriage, the inevitable separation means that each twin follows her own path with emerging differences.

Judy, born first, and twelve hours older, needs people through whom to re-charge her batteries, whereas I am a natural introvert needing solitude to recharge mine.

Even though Judy struggles to grasp a belief system that has come to define my own life, nevertheless she has had moments of astonishing spiritual creativity expressed in some truly beautiful poetry. The first intimation that she had this gift revealed itself in a series of poems penned during the happy years of her marriage to Edward – several of which are reproduced here.

# EVENING

*All around lie petals
slowly fallen,
leaves that have dropped,
flower heads spent.
A thrush stays just long enough
to say 'Goodnight'
and then flies on.
In the garden there is peace,
an air of stillness
unknown in daylight hours.
Leaf and blossom hang together,
tease our memories.
All around a sense of hush.
Blackbirds sing their lullaby,
a choir of Nature's own rare quality.
To the west the sun
is setting,
a slowly rolling band of red
then pink that fades
against a striking branch.
A tree of beauty
it stands majestically against the sky line
then fades away.
It too has gone
until another day.
Lights begin to twinkle
where children sleep,
cats are out,
A walker walks
with stick and dog for company,
windows close.
Another day awaits.*

## SEPTEMBER

*It's finished now*
*the last bud has fallen from the hollyhock,*
*stems are bare*
*where once they bowed*
*and sighed from weight of blooms*
*rich in colour and their velvetness.*
*Now no longer bees can play on them*
*or sway in gentle breeze*
*nor dance again in sunlight.*
*There is a feel of hopelessness,*
*untidiness,*
*as grass begins to fade*
*and leaves turn brown*
*and die.*
*Foxgloves form their seed pods*
*while Dahlias hang their heads*
*and Nasturtiums,*
*that once traversed so far,*
*have now outgrown their strength.*
*Buddleias too form their brown skein*
*against a dew bedecked spider's web*
*while around the shed*
*and on the windows*
*spiders wait.*
*Inside, the potting shed is full of bulbs*
*and precious pots that hopefully will*
*flower again.*
*So we must wait*
*and say 'Goodnight,*
*dear garden – sleep well*
*and wake again for us in Spring.'*

## THE CLEMATIS

*It would not grow.*
*Too shy at first*
*it showed a leaf,*
*Tried to grow but then took fright*
*And hid again.*

*He covered it and talked and nurtured it,*
*Fed it love and bid it try*
*again to grow.*
*'Be brave and show me*
*you can do it.'*

*And now it flowers.*
*Not one*
*but hundreds,*
*A mass of trailing, daring blooms*
*that cover frame*
*up which it grows.*
*A vibrant glow*
*Spread feverishly along the frame.*
*Inquisitive.*
*Proud*
*To prove it can.*

*And then it drops*
*One by one, and settles,*
*A crazy mass of pink.*
*'Well done' he says*
*'I knew you could.'*

## SPRING

*I have not seen a clearer sky*
*Nor greener grass*
    *than that which shows its head just now,*
*Nor brighter hues in daffodil,*
    *or primrose and violet,*
*Heard them say*
*'Did you doubt I would appear?'*


*I have not heard a clearer Lark*
    *that soars so high*
*in sky*
*so blue*
*Near sea that rides and falls on shore*
*And back again.*


*I have not felt a greater joy*
    *now Winter finally has left her coat*
*And hung her dark and dreary cloak*
*And put away her wet and foggy days*
*And sent instead her Sister Spring*
*to bathe us all in light and sun*
*And hope for days not yet begun.*

## IN A SUSSEX CHURCHYARD

*Above an old lychgate a lantern hangs,*
*beside some words which say:*
*'I shall be a light unto your path.'*
*Given with love in gratitude this light*
*will shine for all to see their way*
*when winter nights*
*and rain*
*make it a muddy track.*
*But today the sun is shining*
*and the weeded path leads us along*
*to see what lies beyond.*
*It turns the corner*
*and then breaks out*
*and there below*
*is all of Sussex and beyond.*
*And in the foreground*
*and on the hillside*
*are all the dedications and memories*
*of those beloved gone to rest.*
*A crazy pewter pot lies on its side*
*blown perhaps in gust of Sussex breeze.*
*Fresh flowers lie on some*
*while others have a broken stone*
*or even none at all.*
*A bin of wire stands full to overflowing*
*with wrappings and stalks from roses gone;*
*while in the background*
*close to the church there is a seat*
*now rusting but still firm.*

*How much sorrow has this churchyard seen?*
*But still it stands.*
*A source of strength and comfort*
*to those who seek its peace and solitude.*
*This place is rich memories*
*yet beauty still:*
*A rare and mystic thing*

*cont.*

> *that words alone cannot express.*
> *I could sit here*
> *a long, long time*
> *and never quite identify*
> *the unknown, hidden peace, the purity*
> *that comes from being...*
> *in this Sussex churchyard.*

* * *

Sadly, after her husband's sudden death in 2003, inspiration for writing seemed to drain away and she has not written further poetry since that time.

But despite her insistence that she 'disowns' a belief system and cannot understand my own commitment, nevertheless there was an occasion where it was obvious that deep within her lies the dormant seed, expressed in a truly inspirational way. We were participating in one of Rev. Barry Preece's day retreats at St. Columba's House, Woking, where he had invited each member of the group to choose and then study a card from the pile on a table before us. After studying our cards, we were asked to write a letter to ourselves as if from God. Judy chose a card with beautiful apple blossom and wrote:

> **I am sending you some blossom which I know you will enjoy – take comfort from its beauty – as a reminder of days gone by but also take strength from its delicacy and fragrance and strive to become equal to it – both in all you will now achieve but also in the love you give others on the rest of your journey – so they will remember you in a special way – as you remember this blossom and those who love you.**
>
> **And I am God     3/2/2007**

While Judy is technically the older, I have always felt deeply protective of her and, as identical twins, we have always shared a unique closeness. Judy is blessed with a gentle personality which belies the strength of will underneath and during the course of her life, she has overcome truly enormous problems (mainly financial) that would have defeated and pushed most people under. She was able to run a home on even less than a shoestring – probably the result of being a war baby when our weekly pocket money was one old penny!

But as the years have passed and life has taken us on our separate very different journeys, our husbands have inevitably come between us. Edward became her soulmate, friend and companion but his untimely death in 2003 resulted in a re-awakening of the earlier closeness between us. Michael, my own husband, has never seen the 'Twinship' as a threat to our marital closeness but rather an amazing aspect of being married to a twin!

Of course there are times when tensions surface, but overall, it is a privilege to be Judy's twin and to have this unique bond only identical twins can share.

**Fantasy world**

Another integral part of the Twinship is the fantasy world which originated in our childhood but which still holds true today. When alone together, we revert spontaneously to a secret world of characters, playing out their roles, with different voices, mannerisms and circumstances as prompted by the other – thus the story lines emerge. No script or theme is needed – it just develops as we go along. It makes perfect sense to us but is utterly incomprehensible to anyone else!

However, such a fantasy world is not unknown in other Twinships!

*Childhood twins*

*A little older*

# SECTION III

## The Spiritual Projects

Part I: Cultural Country Retreats

Part II: 'Five Gold Rings',
1st Book, Published 2003

Part III: St. George's House, Windsor Castle

Part IV: 'Symphony of Life',
2nd Book, Published 2009

Part V: Words, Music, Stillness

Part VI: A Cathedral Dream

# I

# CULTURAL COUNTRY RETREATS

One afternoon in the early 1990s, I was sitting at home – very unsettled and dissatisfied with my current working life. I began asking myself:

- What do I enjoy doing?
- What am I good at?
- What is really important to me?

And slowly but very surely, the whole concept of Cultural Country Retreats came into my mind during the course of that afternoon – the name, how it would work and its meaning and purpose. It would be an entirely unique national network of retreats based at key retreat houses across the UK, designed for folk on the fringe of the church, all of whom needed to find a purpose in life – some of whom had probably rejected traditional church life. After all, we all share a common need – to make sense of our lives and where they might be going.

These retreats would have three main elements: a topical, spiritual theme led by experienced retreat conductors gifted with people skills, a cultural element involving a nearby (classical) music festival and all would be set in areas of outstanding natural beauty to allow participants to be refreshed by absorbing the beauty of the English countryside.

Excited by the hope that my vision might become a reality, I set about contacting all Diocesan Anglican Bishops in the UK, seeking firstly, support for the concept and secondly, inviting them to name those in their Diocese who might be interested in leading this new form of retreat. I then sat back and waited!

To my astonishment, the response was overwhelmingly in favour and included such comments as: 'I cannot understand why no-one has tried this before! A wonderful and envisioned idea.'

*The logo for Cultural Country Retreats*

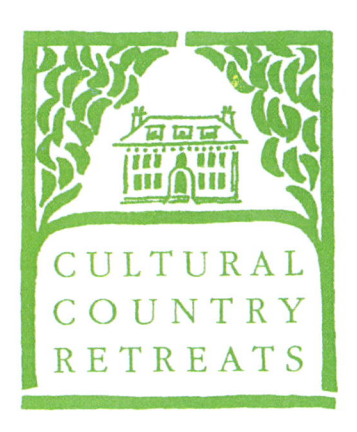

*Piccards Manor - venue for initial meeting of Cultural Country Retreats*

Next I felt it essential to gather together all the folk who had been recommended as potential retreat leaders by the Bishops. Some months later, we had our first gathering at a beautiful country house in Guildford.

Hugely encouraged by the result of that gathering, Michael and I set about planning an exploratory journey up and down the UK, visiting various retreat houses which might make suitable venues for our programme. We contacted a graphic designer for a house-style to be designed for the publicity. We drafted our first year's programme, invited leaders, established an Advisory Board which would meet regularly, appointed a Chairman (Rt. Rev. John Dennis, at that time Bishop of St. Edmundsbury and Ipswich who had warmly supported the concept from its outset), applied for Charitable status, opened a bank account and progressed all the other details involved in establishing a new business.

The first letter posted to all potential supporters nominated by the Bishops, outlined my vision and extracts from this letter are shown below:

> Dear Friend,
>
> ***There has perhaps never been a moment***
> ***when the importance of 'being' is so neglected***
> ***in the general preoccupation with 'doing'***
> ***and when there is no realisation at heart***
> ***of the unfolding of the human spirit***
> ***which the truth demands...***
>
> Sir Laurens van der Post – About Blady
>
> *Cultural Country Retreats represents a new concept in essential short breaks, designed to allow men and women from all walks of life to draw back for a while, take stock of their lives and through the medium of culture (visits to National Trust Properties and places of historical interest, music festivals, choral and orchestral concerts) walking and time for spiritual thought and reflection, reassess priorities. The idea centres around establishing retreats for those who might not normally consider this type of break as well as those for whom retreats are a valuable part of their lives. The aim is to promote and co-ordinate already established facilities in what may prove to be a totally unique way.*

*Cultural Country Retreats will be based in specially selected retreat houses throughout Great Britain. Each retreat will be led by an experienced Retreat Director and the optional activities will include opportunities for spiritual reflection, group and private discussion, guided walks, visits to National Trust properties and music festivals where appropriate. The concept will be open to people of all faiths or none.*

*Cultural Country Retreats has the warm support of bishops and other church leaders throughout Great Britain, the National Trust, many retreat directors and retreat houses and of individuals including Sir Laurens van der Post, Fr Gerard Hughes SJ and many others who have welcomed the concept with enthusiasm.*

*Yours Sincerely*

Gradually a substantial mailing list was established and the first programme printed and posted out. The response was hugely encouraging and we forged ahead with plans for future programmes.

We introduced a regular Newsletter, an annual reunion of those who had attended previous retreats and we posted a Christmas card to all on our mailing list. The Advisory Board met regularly to keep a watchful eye and make suggestions as appropriate.

The retreat houses we found to be most popular included:

### Holland House in Cropthorne, Pershore, Worc
A superb half-timbered building, quietly tucked away in Cropthorne with idyllic gardens sloping down to the river Avon.

### Parcevall Hall, Appletreewick, Yorkshire
One of my absolute favourites, an impressive building with spreading views across the valley and hills, offering an amazing almost tangible welcome.

### Isaac Walton Hotel, Derbyshire
A brave choice – our first hotel – which, because of its position over Dovedale, proved to be a popular choice.

### Brook Place, Chobham, Surrey
Another superlative venue with its attractive Jacobean House with acres of immaculate grounds.

### *Belmont Abbey, Hereford*
A beautifully refurbished retreat house linked to the Abbey.

The key retreat themes and leaders included:

**Becoming What We Are – Midlife & Beyond**
Canon Bruce Duncan

**Windows On Reality**
Rev. Barry Preece

**Life Goals**
Rev. John Gordon Clark

**Pilgrimage**
Canon Bruce Duncan

**Stillness and Stress**
Wanda Nash

**Increasing Awareness – Daring To Be**
Dr. Alwyn Marriage

**Security Alert!**
Rev. Canon Dr. Maureen Palmer

**The Challenge of Change**
Canon Bruce Duncan

**Today's Ethical Minefield – How Do We Cope?**
Rev. Canon Dr. Maureen Palmer

**Walking the Tightrope – Competing Claims on our Lives**
Rev. Prebendary Michael Shrewsbury

**From Where......to Where?**
Rt. Rev. John Dennis

**A New Spirituality for a New Millennium**
Rev. Adrian Smith

*Parcevall Hall, North Yorkshire*

*Anna, beside the front entrance of Parcevall Hall, North Yorkshire*

*Holland House, Pershore*

The Music Festivals that were top favourites included:

- Harrogate Festival
- Brighton Festival
- Buxton Festival
- Three Choirs Festival, Hereford
- Three Choirs Festival, Gloucester

Through all these years we were running Cultural Country Retreats, we received some wonderfully encouraging letters of thanks including:

### Sir Laurens van der Post:
'I am so glad your plans for CCR are being fulfilled. I wish you God speed for what I'm certain will be an immensely creative venture in the lives of all who participate.'

### A grateful retreatant:
'What makes your endeavour, I think, so laudable and worthy of support is that we live in a world where the sheer 'busyness' inflicted on us makes retreats of the kind you arrange, a necessity. They are indispensable as a kind of inner fortress against the elements of fragmentation which enclose us all.'

### Fr. Gerard W. Hughes SJ:
'I congratulate you on the idea and am sure it will flourish.'

### Rev Canon Bruce Duncan: Sarum College:
'As you are obviously aware, there is an enormous spiritual hunger in our society today which is being met only partially by traditional church activities. Your concept of CCR strikes me as a very imaginative and worthwhile extension of the retreat movement which I am sure will help meet some of the spiritual needs of many people who for various reasons, might not contemplate a more traditional retreat.'

### Assistant Bishop of Bradford
'I am aware that there is an increasing desire on the part of many people to escape from a materialistically-minded consumer society – these people will, I am sure, benefit from your retreats. I applaud your initiative.'

**Bishop's House, Norwich**
*'I am amazed no one has thought of it before!'*

**Rt. Rev. John Dennis, Bishop of St. Edmundsbury & Ipswich**
*'Cultural Country Retreats is a new approach for the stressed and for the searching. It is for those who need time to catch up with themselves. It is imaginative, fresh and different and it has already proved itself in practice.'*

**Bishop of Salisbury:**
*'Anything that will encourage a new tranche of people to pause, reflect and be – is a great blessing.'*

In subsequent years while our programmes were flourishing, letters of appreciation continued to pour in from those who had participated in our retreats:

*'For me, it had a perfect balance of everything I love: music, art, literature, nature, history, exploring our faith and last but not least – peace! Everything was organised to perfection...'*

*'I should like to express my deep appreciation for the weekend at Brook Place – the group was excellent and stimulating as was our leader. The meeting together of different people with various spiritual experiences was very widening and encouraging.'*

*'I loved our visit to the Three Choirs Festival in Gloucester Cathedral. An inspiring building and when full to bursting with sound and light – almost overwhelming – yet another lovely memory to take away.'*

*'I was so glad to see how CCR has prospered and developed in these past two years. You and Michael must be very pleased about it all and your hopes and plans for the future of which you spoke, sound very perceptive and possible.'*

*'I look back on the retreat at Holland House with great pleasure. I thought John Dennis was inspired as Conductor and it was such a treat to listen to the intelligent and mature*

*participants. Thank you so much for enabling us to attend the magnificent concert at Gloucester Cathedral.'*

*'Thank you for all your hard work in organising such a lovely weekend with its perfect balance and elegant surroundings – excellent food, wonderful music and profound spirituality.'*

*'I have been humming bits of the Elgar ever since I left and reflecting on my good fortune in knowing about CCR. I personally appreciated the space that was left around the sessions, the good timekeeping and the unobtrusive way in which you bonded the group.'*

*'I had such a marvellous time at Parcevall Hall and feel so refreshed. It was such a fantastically reviving experience.'*

*'Thank you for all your hard work and inspiration which goes into the organisation of CCR.'*

The aims and objectives of Cultural Country Retreats were:

*To encourage the development of faith in God in individuals and society*

*To enable men and women to consider questions of faith and to discover those values which are central to self-understanding and to the place of the individual in the society of today and tomorrow*

*To provide an opportunity for the renewal of faith and the consequent transformation of life*

*To enable men and women to look constructively and creatively at human uniqueness and mortality within the providence of God*

*To give men and women an opportunity of seeking inspiration and a wider vision so that their work and daily lives may be of greater value*

*To enable those in positions of leadership and influence to come to a new and deeper understanding of their moral*

> *responsibilities towards those whom they serve and work amongst*
>
> *To enable men and women to mature into the kind of human beings God alone knows they have the potential to become*
>
> *To provide an opportunity for a review of the value of prayer, of the power of the spirit and the spiritual dimension of life in a world of conflict and change*

Through

> *The opportunity to draw apart from the preoccupation and pressures of their daily lives, for renewal, in a place of quiet*
>
> *The opportunity for walking in areas of natural beauty in order to promote physical, spiritual and mental refreshment*
>
> *A cultural framework provided by music and the arts within which spiritual reflection can take place under the direction and guidance of experienced retreat leaders*
>
> *The renewed practice of prayer and the sacramental life in the context of the Christian faith*

However, after nearly ten years of running CCR, the pressures of directing such an organisation involving so much attention to detail, careful liaison with all bodies involved, and all the research and administration for our yearly programmes – all this whilst undertaking a full-time demanding post in education – it was with great reluctance that I came to realise that it was time to pause and reflect on the project. Additionally, some of the key centres we used were closing as major changes were themselves engulfing retreat houses and thus we delayed further programme planning until we had had an opportunity to consider a different style and format for CCR – at some point in the future.

* * *

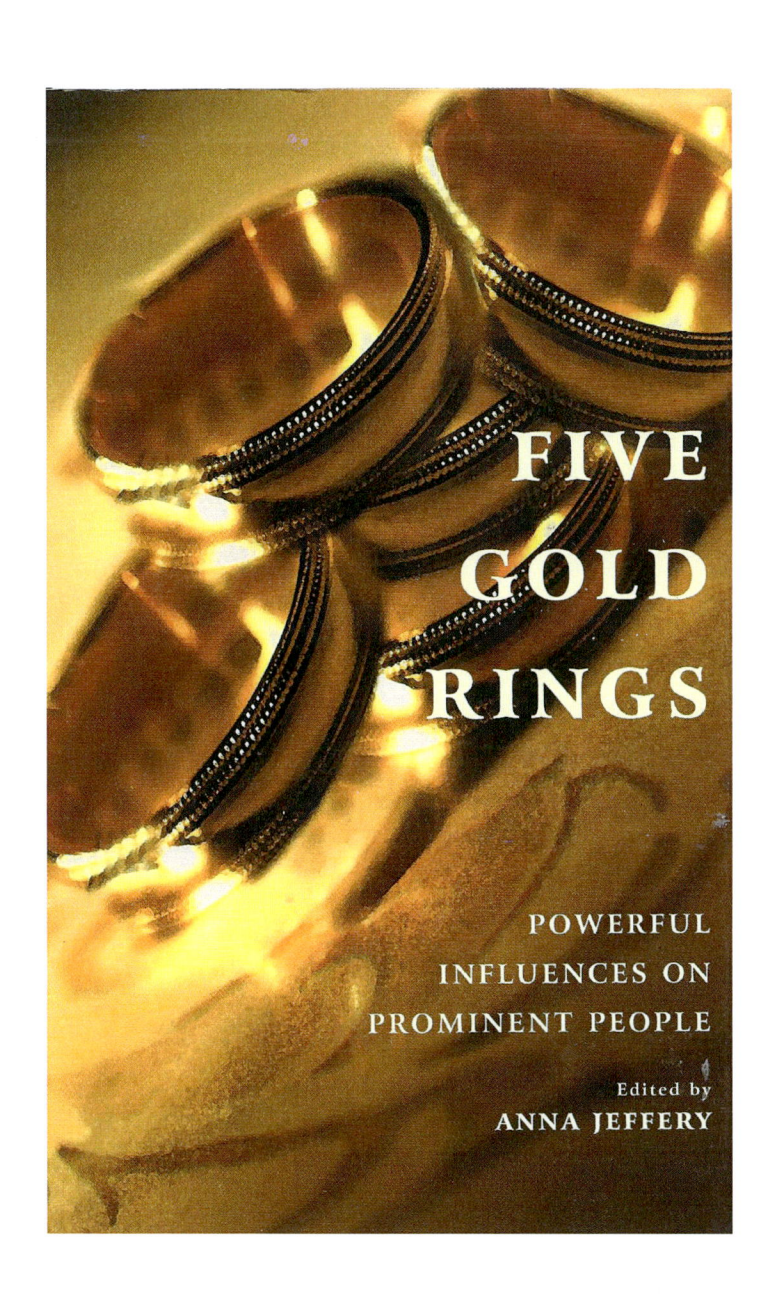

# FIVE GOLD RINGS

## POWERFUL INFLUENCES ON PROMINENT PEOPLE

Edited by
ANNA JEFFERY

# II

# FIVE GOLD RINGS

'Five Gold Rings' - a book published by Darton, Longman and Todd in 2003 – marked my first foray into publishing.

It began in the early months of the new millennium when the idea of inviting well known figures to identify five areas of influence that had impacted their lives – and thus their faith journey – began to stir within me. The five areas of influence would be:

>  The person -
>  The book -
>  The place -
>  The poem -
>  And lastly, their philosophy of life

These together would represent their 'Five Gold Rings'.

I found myself reflecting on questions such as:

>  What makes people?
>  What helps to shape and form their lives?
>  Could it be a particular person?
>  A book?
>  A place of special significance or meaning?
>  Some haunting lines of poetry?
>  How open and receptive are we to God's guiding hand through such profound influences?

These questions prompted my search for prominent people who were willing to reveal their Five Gold Rings as outlined above.

After much research, which led me to approach Bishops, medical personnel, writers, scientists, senior theologians and others, I finally achieved a list of 23 contributors. Fascinating portraits emerged through these frank confessions. Ultimately readers were encouraged to search for their own Five Gold Rings in order to recognise the golden thread of guidance running through their lives – as it has through my own.

As a new writer, finding a publisher was more challenging but a breakthrough came via a colleague, – Father Robert Llewelyn, and I was delighted when Darton, Longman and Todd accepted the MS and were happy to publish the book in 2003.

Abbreviated extracts from the writings of key contributors include the following:

**Rt. Rev. Simon Barrington-Ward:**

*The Person: Viola Garvin*

My parents surely shaped my mind and heart and gave me a framework of values underpinned by a sense of God but it was Viola Garvin, 'Aunt' Viola to me, who loomed gently over my childhood and youth – she added to life another vivid dimension of a kind of mystery and presence. Saying on one occasion: 'Simon, you are like God, your silences are so immense; your communications so delightful!' She introduced me to Julian of Norwich and talked of love and forgiveness. She showed me what it means 'to live with vision, courage and no hate!'

*The Book: The Brothers Karamazov by Dostoevsky*

The story presents vividly what for me has seemed since my Berlin time, the underlying and crucial drama of our time, our need and struggle for that true social and spiritual reality we can only find in God, a reality opened up to us in those people who genuinely reflect Christ.

Dostoevsky gives us a glimpse of the future which purified hearts alone can bring in. For me certainly, as for his contemporaries and many since, Dostoevsky has made this wholeness through brokenness, this alternative to the terrible fate hanging over humanity and creation itself, lastingly compelling.

*The Place: Berlin 1953*

Here I met with Christians in East and West and went with them to the opera. Among them I began to discern the person of Christ as 'God with and for us'. He became the root of a flowering in the winter city, a way beyond East and West, a movement in his Spirit of breaking and re-making life through death, growth through forgiven-ness into love, which Berlin, like Dresden later in my life, would always symbolise for me.

*The Poem: That Nature is a Heraclitean Fire and of the comfort of the Resurrection – Gerard Manley Hopkins*

When I was leaving school and my father died, I first read this poem and was overwhelmed by it and realised how deeply it spoke to me of the way in which the tragic transience and ebbing away of life alone can be countered.

In this poem it is also a kind of transcending of nature, a resistance which shines out against the dark that opens up the promise of a new destiny for the whole creation.

*My Philosophy of Life*

Ultimately we need to discover together and each in our own heart that fusion of homecoming and journeying, contemplation and intercession, joyful mourning, being at peace and yet longing and working for peace for all, being 'still and still moving' which is the secret of great literature, great art, and great music... so the love which holds us is also the love which draws us ever deeper and further into the redemptive process in this world and in the world to come.

**Father Laurence Freeman**

*The Person: John Main*

I first met John Main when I was a boy at school. He had a self-evident authority and genuine ease of self-assurance. I think it was recognition at a level deeper than reason or emotion of a person who would later give my life specific depth and direction. In the East it is a more common experience, the recognition of your guru.

John Main occupies a place in my life and identity undiminished by time and strangely strengthened by death. His deep and solitary detachment was the human space in which Christ the true teacher, the centre of every centre, really began to be formed in me.

*The Book: The Book of the Gospels*

This is the book that has most influenced me and continues to do so. Of the four gospels, John is the glory, the most mystical and most human. In John especially we imagine or see Jesus laughing and weeping. Within John it is the resurrection appearances that make me feel that this book, although it may not have been the last book to be written, will be the last to be understood.

*The Place: New College, Oxford*

As I was waiting for my admission result I had a dream of walking in some hills and seeing in the far distance a lovely city glowing in a golden light. For a while and so in a sense for life, Oxford was that city for me. The dream recurs occasionally, sometimes in real life, especially when an epiphany is about to happen or to close. Where the real city, the New Jerusalem, is to be found is the question and the journey that New College helped me to get started on.

*The Poem: Love – George Herbert*

This is a poem of infinite tenderness, not less than the divine unconditional love. But it is set against a background of bitter, self-induced suffering. The struggle between God and ego is fiercer than that between flesh and spirit. One may hardly notice the darkness in the poem as the light is so much stronger.

*My Philosophy of Life*

I don't know if I have a philosophy of life. However I do have a preferred way of life and the best expression of its ideal is the Rule of St. Benedict. The timeless wisdom and adaptability of the Rule is its sense of measure, moderation in all things.

Prayer, work and study correspond in his vision to the tripartite harmony of the human person which is spirit, body and mind. They are indivisible yet distinct, interweaving yet autonomous. The anxiety and violence of much modern life arises from their being arrhythmic and unbalanced. This is most critically seen in the problem of stress that is so destructive and yet is often not much more than the failure to measure our time properly and to respect one's whole self.

Benedict's vision is all about balance in daily life leading to peace of soul and thus to a just society.

**Rt. Rev. Michael Marshall**

*The Person: Eric Abbot, former Dean of Westminster*

For many years, Eric served as my spiritual director – there was always more light in the room where Eric was; more fun and godly merriment as with gentle teasing he would help you to say and share things about yourself that you never thought you could ever share with anybody.

Eric had through contemplative prayer – the prayer of the heart – transformed merely intellectual knowledge and information into that higher form of knowledge, best expressed as love. This was perhaps most evident in his style of preaching which warmed the heart and fired the will. Eric brought out the best in people as a pastor, a preacher and priest. Both the church and the world were colder for me and countless others, the day Eric died.

And his secret? He had discovered what it was and is to be essentially human – warts and all. He refused to be daunted by massive failures in others because one must assume that he was first in touch with his own and yet also discovered the sufficiency of God's grace as the unqualified remedy for the human tragedy.

### *The Book: Confessions by St. Augustine*

Undoubtedly the book that has had the greatest effect upon my life is Confessions by St. Augustine.

It was Laurens van der Post who once said: 'If you haven't a story to tell, you haven't a life to live.' Augustine's story is a story worth telling and retelling about a life that eventually was truly and supremely a life worth living. His story unashamedly tells of his struggles and failures; of a journey for much of which he was running away from God. For the first 33 years of his life, Augustine shopped around the supermarket of the religious options of his day. His personal life was driven by rampant ambition and pride, expressed through reckless and tortuous relationships. Eventually his life fell apart in what we would nowadays call a breakdown. Yet it is precisely at the point of breakdown that God breaks through.

In so many ways I have discovered an uncanny resonance between Augustine's story and my own. It takes a lifetime and more to realise fully that it is the free unearned gift of grace and that grace alone can save us from ourselves, from both our strengths and weaknesses and furthermore that when we offer our weaknesses to God, he and he alone can transform them into real and authentic strengths.

### *The Place: the Protestant Community of Taize, France*

I stumbled across the Protestant Community of Taize in France in the sixties, shortly after ordination. As I climbed the hill up to the 'Church of Reconciliation at Taize', I discovered the power of transcendent worship as a converting experience.

God is essentially 'persons-in-community' and in so far as we are made in God's image we come to the fullness of our humanity when we discover our place in community and in the communion of saints.

Taize is for me, as for so many others, the place of encounter and what I might want to call holistic Christianity. Throughout history disciples have always needed shrines and holy places, somewhere, so that as God's spies they can go out and discover, recover and uncover that same glory of God *everywhere*.

*The Poem: Love (III) by George Herbert*
It has taken me a lifetime and 40 years of gospel ministry – yet only latterly have I begun to come perhaps somewhere near the insight of George Herbert as he expresses it in this poem.

*My Philosophy of Life*
'All will be well; all manner of things will be well' Dame Julian of Norwich

This sums up the philosophy of life for that remarkable fourteenth-century mystic. At the first take, such an overriding outlook on life in our tragic world might appear to be bland and out of touch with the pain and grief of the human story.

What, we might well ask, was this optimistic philosophy of life based upon in the real world either of the first century, the fourteenth century or in the world of our own day?

Yet it is the belief in a God who has brought and continues to bring good out of evil, as was so powerfully and dramatically manifested in the cross and resurrection of Jesus, which enables us to replace despair with that deeply Christian virtue of hope.

## Rev. Dr. John Polkinghorne

*The Person: Eric Hutchison – Canadian priest*
I would like to pay grateful tribute to someone who has had an important, if somewhat hidden influence on the more public side of my life – Eric Hutchison, Canadian priest and Jungian psychotherapist.

I learned many significant things from Eric but one of the most important was his way of exploring the Bible that was open to its spiritual power in a way that expanded rather than narrowed one's thinking. Our friendship and many conversations together, helped me to see how theological thinking exceeds even scientific thinking in its insightful power to yield understanding of reality. His influence played a significant part in motivating my eventual decision to seek ordination.

*The Book: The Crucified God: Jurgen Moltmann*

During the time prior to ordination, Keith Sutton, then Principal of Ridley Hall, suggested I ought to read 'some serious theology' as he put it, before beginning my formal training. He suggested I started with The Crucified God.

In doing so I was bowled over by the creative power of theological thinking that the book displayed. I do not claim that his insight removes all the perplexity and anguish that we feel in the face of suffering for example, but it does meet it at the very deep level that the problem demands.

*The Place: Cambridge*

Cambridge is a city of great beauty, with its many ancient college buildings. My last job was as President of Queens' College so we lived in the President's Lodge – it was an enormous privilege to have such a splendid house as one's home.

Cambridge is certainly a heritage city but it is not at all in thrall to the past, being perpetually and intellectually lively in its continuing life.

It has been a great privilege to have spent so much of my life in this East Anglian city of plain living and high thinking.

*The Poem: Love Bade Me Welcome: George Herbert*

George Herbert, a Fellow of Trinity College, Cambridge, seems to me to be the perfect example of devout but moderate Anglican piety and this well-known poem with its moving portrayal of Christ graciously greeting the hesitant sinner – is undoubtedly my favourite.

*My Philosophy of Life*

The centre of my life and the ground on which I seek to base my approach to living, is my Christian faith.

Central to my Christian faith is the figure of Christ – no philosophy of life could be satisfactory for me that did not take Jesus fully into account. He is a compelling figure, even if in some ways a mysterious figure.

The fundamental Christian assertion that 'Jesus lives' – for me centres on the Eucharistic worship of the church. It is not easy to express all of this adequately but here I find the focus of my spiritual life and the place of meeting with the One I seek to acknowledge as the Lord of my life.

**Sir Mark Tully**

*The Person: Philip Francis*

There have been so many people who have influenced my life that it is very difficult to choose one person. However, the person who influenced me most deeply was the vicar of the small country church I attended during school holidays – Philip Francis – of All Saints Marthall, Knutsford. No one could call Philip a prominent churchman and that is what impressed me most. What attracted me was his perseverance in the faith without looking for any reward. Philip's example led me to believe that the peace of God can never be found by those who lack humility, by those who aspire for greatness.

Philip believed in fulfilling his vocation as well as he could, leaving rewards and judgement to God. I could not claim to have lived up to his example but, in my ego-bruising profession, whenever my ego has been bruised I have thought of Philip.

*The Book: The Book of Common Prayer*

The book I return to time and time again is not the Bible but The Book of Common Prayer – the Collects are especially meaningful – I am reminded that I cannot do anything which is good without God – together with the fact that God is 'always more ready to hear than we are to pray'.

The liturgy also became an essential part of my life when I was young – my love of the liturgy is not rational, I don't want to examine the wonderful words too closely. They are beautiful and mysterious, as God is.

*The Place: Chail, a small town in the western Himalayas*

At 2226 metres above sea level, Chail is high enough to provide awe-inspiring views of the snow-capped peaks and the foothills of the Himalayas, ridge after ridge rolling down to the great Gangetic plain. No photograph or film can capture the many-coloured monsoon sunsets – they have to be seen to be believed. The scent of pine forests is purer than any perfume. To become part of the mountains, I need time to change, to relearn the art of peaceful living – a day outing is not enough. At Chail, both mighty mountains and a stormy sea fill me with a sense of my unimportance. They dwarf any human achievement. They are primeval, far older than we are. We can deface the mountains with our constructions and indeed destruction but somehow their majesty remains.

When I stand beside a small Hindu shrine on a mountaintop above the forests of Chail I do indeed feel very small but I become aware that I am not without significance. I belong, I am part of nature and have my place too.

*The Poem: God's Grandeur, Gerard Manley Hopkins*
The Jesuit priest's poem starts: 'The world is charged with the grandeur of God.' It is God who charges the world with the energy that upholds it – an energy without which all the energy we generate and use would be of no avail, the world would fall apart. But as a Christian, the poet cannot despair, he must have faith in God's mercy and his power.

*My Philosophy of Life*
To say that I have a philosophy of life would suggest that I have found all the answers to living. I haven't. I believe that life is one long search and that we will never reach certainty. What we can strive for is to find a path through life but that means reading the signs along the way, being open-minded.

How does one live with uncertainty? A Hindu friend of mine has suggested that balance is the key. A balance has to be sought between certainty and uncertainty.

One of the most important balancing acts we are called upon to perform, is to balance fate with the free will to choose. That is one of the most important balancing acts we are called to perform – to accept fate without becoming fatalists, to accept free will without coming to believe we are entirely in charge of our own destiny. I must acknowledge the need for balance between fate and free will, accepting that I am like a tight-rope walker always in danger of losing my balance. I have come to the conclusion that life has to be a continuous search for balance rather than the stationary stability of certainty which is stagnation.

**Rt. Hon. the Lord Weatherill**

*The Person: My mother*
My mother was born in 1886 and by contrast to my father was highly educated and cultured. She attended Leipzig University in 1904 and subsequently trained as a nurse in Bart's Hospital. She was formidable, strict but kind and had far reaching effects on my life.

*The Book: Emerson's Essays*

There have been many masters of wisdom but Emerson has the gift of an interpreter – his essays on self-reliance, compensation, manners, character and, above all, love have helped to shape my life.

*The Place: India*

Without a doubt – India. As soon as I stepped ashore in Bombay in 1940 I felt at home.

Today I am a firm believer in reincarnation and I am in no doubt that this was the reason.

In Northern India in 1942 I came across a tomb bearing the inscription: 'He was trusted – absolutely.' This memory came to me out of the blue shortly after I was elected Speaker of the Commons in 1983 and I adopted it as my motto. I pray that I lived up to it.

*The Poem: A Creed by John Masefield*

I believe that each incarnation is a training ground for the next, until we reach Nirvana – union with God. In the words of John Masefield:

*I hold that when a person dies*
*His soul returns again to earth*
*Arrayed in some new flesh-disguise –*
*Another mother gives him birth.*
*With sturdier limbs and brighter brain*
*The old soul takes the road again.*

*My Philosophy of Life*

My philosophy throughout the forty years in parliament has been shaped by Mahatma Gandhi's 'Seven Social Sins':

*Politics without principles*
*Wealth without work*
*Pleasure without conscience*
*Knowledge without character*
*Commerce without morality*
*Science without humanity*
*Worship without sacrifice*

## Rt. Rev. Richard Harries

*The Person: My mother*

I believe that in my early days, months and years, I was warmly embraced, affirmed and cherished. Nothing later in life could compare with this influence which has given me a sense of my own identity and worth.

*The Book: Dostoevsky's The Brothers Karamazov*

This wrestles, as no other book does with the fundamental issue of evil and suffering, and how, if at all, they can be reconciled with belief in a loving God. It set an agenda which is still with us.

*The Place: Burford Priory*

This is an Anglican religious community where the worship is simple but beautiful, at once highly disciplined and sincere. The setting is miraculous and is a place I value greatly for quiet days.

*The Poem: T.S. Eliot's Four Quartets*

This faces the bleakness of so much life but it also suggests that there is something beyond emptiness at 'The still point of the turning world.' Its haunting imagery and rhythms continue to reverberate in the mind.

*My Philosophy of Life*

As far as my philosophy of life is concerned, I take seriously the fact that God has given the world a real independence. Because he respects the freedom he has given the world as a whole and human choices in particular, he does not perform the miracles we so often long for.

But God is working all the time to bring good out of evil. His purpose is not simply to increase pleasure and diminish pain, important though these are, but to help us grow in our capacity to love. Because this love comes in the end from God himself, what is rooted in love cannot be destroyed. So life points beyond itself to its consummation in the communion of saints.

\* \* \*

Reviewers were generous in their acclamation including:

> I found this book really captivating and inspirational. The choice of almost two dozen well known and in most cases much loved Public Figures who were persuaded to reveal so

much of themselves must be the work of a very special and gifted person. I cannot recommend this book too highly as I enjoyed it from beginning to end...

(www.thegoodbookstall.org.uk)

We launched 'Five Gold Rings' in Guildford Cathedral soon after completion, with most of the contributors present, in the presence of the Very Rev. Alex Wedderspoon, then Dean, Rev. Canon Dr. Maureen Palmer, Sub-Dean, representative from the publishers, Darton Longman and Todd and a host of friends and invited guests. It was indeed a happy occasion.

Today, sales of 'Five Gold Rings' continue through Amazon. This was indeed an encouraging start to my foray into publishing. Where would that golden thread lead me next?

\* \* \*

# III

# ST. GEORGE'S HOUSE WINDSOR CASTLE

During the ten years or so I spent in London, I developed an absorbing hobby – applying for jobs on an almost weekly basis! If I didn't receive at least one offer regularly, I felt I was losing my touch! Not that I was unhappy in my work, organising educational conferences up and down the country and occasionally abroad, but I just couldn't resist all the challenging opportunities that were available in and around London!

And it was a particularly enticing advertisement that captured my attention one day:

Housekeeper wanted for
St. George's House
Windsor Castle
Full-time live-in post
Flat available

I duly applied, was invited to visit, and after being short-listed, to my great astonishment, was offered the post. A truly once-in-a-lifetime opportunity to work within the castle walls, helping to run this prestigious conference centre.

Nevertheless, many questions opened up in my mind. Was it really for me? Was it too precarious – losing my London flat, losing my social freedom that a live-in post would mean and other major considerations facing someone single, hoping for marriage at some point? Time was not exactly on my side in that respect...

After several sleepless nights, I decided that the time was not right and after much heart-searching, declined the offer, only to have the Dean of Windsor on the phone several times subsequently – almost imploring me to change my mind!

But my decision had been made and thus it was.

However, in spite of the fact that I declined the post, I was invited to act as rapporteur at several subsequent conferences at the house, an experience that was hugely memorable.

And St. George's House eventually featured again in my life, some years later when I was running Cultural Country Retreats. It occurred to me that the House would make an ideal centre for one of these events with its cultural heritage, the splendour of St. George's Chapel, Windsor itself, quite apart from the Great Park and the Saville Gardens, all of which had the hallmarks of a superb weekend.

On a brief historical note, St. George's House was founded in 1966 by H.R.H. The Duke of Edinburgh and the then Dean of Windsor, Robin Woods, as a place where people of influence and responsibility in every part of society, could come together to explore and communicate their views and analysis of contemporary issues.

The House, located within Windsor Castle, formed part of the fourteenth century foundations of the College of St. George. The heart of the College is St. George's Chapel where three times a day, every day, prayer is offered for the nation. It is precisely this tradition of prayer that gives the house its impetus and its wider theological context. The offering of prayer in the chapel finds a practical expression in consultations, where the house today still offers space for nurturing wisdom.

The consultation programme at St. George's House focuses on three distinct areas: contemporary issues, service to the Church and hospitality for groups who, understanding the ethos and core objectives of the house, bring to the house their own consultations. Taken together the annual programme is varied, rich and intellectually challenging.

I duly contacted the then Warden, putting my proposal to him, referring of course to their earlier employment offer, and enclosing details of Cultural Country Retreats. As an Associate of St. George's House from earlier years, I felt I was in a reasonably strong position to make this approach.

I was invited to meet him and absolutely delighted to receive his approval, and subsequently, with the blessing of their Council, we were on course to run a Heritage Break at St. George's House during April 2005. This would include periods of debate and reflection on topical issues, a visit to the State Apartments, attendance at services in St. George's Chapel, visits to places of interest in and around Windsor Castle, a concert and time for reflection.

Rev Canon Dr. Maureen Palmer, Sub-Dean of Guildford Cathedral was able to lead this Heritage Break, using the theme: 'Towards a New Morality' and a summary of her sessions is shown below:

**Towards a New Morality**

Four lectures delivered at St. George's House, Windsor Castle on 8th, 9th, & 10th April 2005 by Rev. Canon Dr. Maureen Palmer

**(1) Why do we need a new morality?**

a: In Western culture, the moral system has its foundations in the Judeo-Christian faith – seeing the behaviour of human beings in the light of the true destiny of what it means to be human and in the vision of God.

b: Morality and ethics are not stable: both systems depend upon deepening of knowledge and technical advances from one generation to another.

c: We traced the background of morality/ethics from Augustine, to Aquinas, to Kant, to Bentham.

d: We need the new morality because we have changed from a 'corporate' view of the world to one which values autonomy, freedom and choice and where the rights of the individual are paramount. It is becoming a morality unfettered by the baggage of history and community.

**(2) Morality in Family Life**

a: There is still the tension of earlier times concerning childlessness. Whereas in Biblical times and indeed until the eighteenth century, childlessness was always seen as the failure of the woman to conceive. Children were important as heirs, as those who would carry the name.

b: In the Book of Common Prayer the Marriage Service set the priorities: procreation, remedy against sin, mutual care and love.

c: There is a new morality of marriage based on sexuality and personhood, contraception, status of women and easier divorce. In recent times too there has been a rise in pornography and explicit sex and associated violence, as well as sex education of the young which has made young people sophisticated though not mature.

d: The Marriage Service in Common Worship has changed the priorities to: trust and love, delight in sexual union, children.

e: Marriage is under pressure, for life expectancy is now much longer and so marriages continue for much longer; we are a population which values instant fulfilment; women are now expected to have careers and are therefore delaying having children.

f: We spoke of what it means to 'beget' children and the effect on this that contraception, IVF and termination of pregnancy has had.

### (3) Morality in Medicine

a: The expectations of patients is now greater – we expect full health for all.

b: The role of the GP has changed – he/she is now 'Mr. Fixit'.

c: There have been many advances in medicine: discovery of DNA; the Human Genome Project which could individualize medicine; the possibility of Screening for Genetic disorders with all the insurance and privacy implications that that could bring. This led us on to discuss cloning and the possible medical use of stem-cell replacement of tissues.

d: Underlying the changes in technology comes the demand for respect for the embryo and a consideration of life as a gift.

### (4) Morality in the Work Place

a: The gift of work: the need to earn; a means to an end; compulsive element of life; dignity of work.

b: Business Ethics: microethics – exchange between individuals with the promise, intentions and successes and failures; macroethics – the business world of justice, market forces and government.

c: Issues of justice; debt; fairness; stewardship; freedom.

d: Global destiny: demands which leave many in the Third World poorer; damage to local economies and local environments.

\* \* \*

The weekend also included Choral Evensong in St. George's Chapel on two evenings, a tour of the chapel, visit to the State Apartments, and an informal concert.

And by some quirk of fate – and a fact that was highly confidential until a few days before our planned Heritage Break – we were informed that the marriage of the Prince of Wales to Camilla Parker Bowles would take place the very weekend we were resident in St. George's House! Thus it was that as the happy couple emerged onto the steps of St. George's Chapel, our group rushed to the window of a nearby building in The Close – to get the best possible view!

\* \* \*

*St. George's House, Windsor Castle*

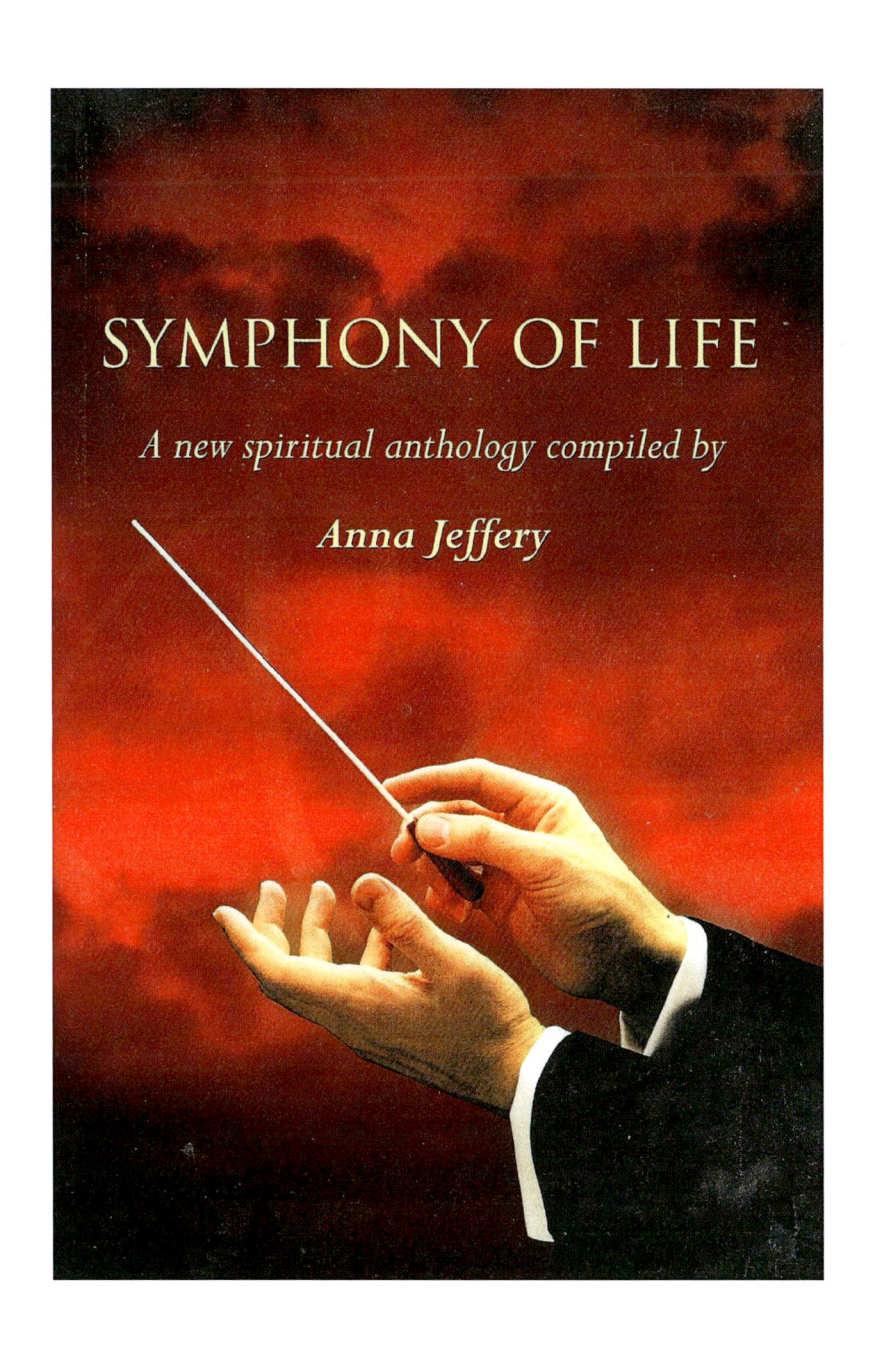

# SYMPHONY OF LIFE

*A new spiritual anthology compiled by*

*Anna Jeffery*

# IV

# SYMPHONY OF LIFE

'Symphony of Life' – my second book, began as a motley collection of writings gathered over the years – mostly while on retreat – but each of which had a special significance for me.

Some years ago, early in 2008, the thought came to me that I should arrange them in book form – taking the shape of a symphony – with each 'movement' representing a stage of our spiritual growth. To my enormous delight and personal satisfaction, the book was published in 2009. Here is how the 'movements' fell into place:

**Prelude**
Beginning/early awareness of God

**1st Movement: Allegro moderato**
The steady influence of God

**2nd Movement: Adagio tranquillo**
When God seems silent

**3rd Movement: Tempestosa**
When life is tough / problematic

**4th Movement: Finale**
End of life/journey's end

Very Rev. Alex Wedderspoon, former Dean of Guildford, wrote in his Foreword:

> 'Music is a strange thing: I would almost say it is a miracle, for it stands half way between spirit and matter: we do not know what music is: it is part of the world of mystery.' So wrote Henrich Heine and there have always been those who have recognised something of the transcendent about music and its composition. 'Mozart', wrote Goethe 'is a human incarnation of the divine creative power.' And he went on to

write: 'I have my own particular sorrows, loves, delights and you have yours. But sorrow, gladness, yearning, hope, love, belong to all of us in all times and all places. Music is the only means whereby we feel these emotions in their universality for music is the common language of all humanity.' So it is entirely appropriate that Anna Jeffery should present this wonderful anthology in the context of a musical theme.

And as I said in my introduction to 'Symphony of Life', life surely is a symphony with its ups and downs – dark phrases and lighter ones with glorious uplands of magical harmonies that lift the spirit to realms of the ethereal; this concept formed the structure to what I hoped would be an uplifting and unusual anthology.

In the same way that a conductor cannot force members of the orchestra to follow his baton, so God cannot force us to follow Him. But those who do find the resultant harmony in their lives to be truly inspirational, rather than the discord heard by those who reject a valid belief system.

'Symphony of Life' is an anthology of other men's insights, other men's inspirations and we need all that they give in order that we might make sense of those difficult, obscure parts of the symphony when God seems silent or the storm clouds gather or the desert unending. We need their awareness, their perception, their understanding so that we too can perceive, understand, pick up the theme of the symphony in the still, silent centre of our souls. Then and only then are we lifted into the heights of joy as we become aware of God - immanent and transcendent.

It was written as a book to inspire at a time when many have questions but few have answers, when many doubt and many more despair, a time when all of us face an uncertain future. It set out to lead the wary, encourage the doubtful and calm the fearful.

Here are some of my favourite pieces:

> Prayer is our humble answer to the inconceivable surprise of living. It is all we can offer in return for the mystery by which we live.
>
> **Abraham Joshua Heschel**

> All life is music, wherein is set all measures and all tones. We are building up a symphony of life – a symphony to God and

higher and higher will we reach until we catch the melody of the angels

**From the Gold of Dawn, source unknown**

Music is a moral law. It gives a soul to the universe,
wings to the mind,
flight to the imagination, a charm to sadness, gaiety and life to everything. It is the essence of order, and leads to all
that is good, just
and beautiful, of which it is the invisible, but
nevertheless dazzling,
passionate and eternal form

**Plato**

The joy of life is living it and doing things of worth,
In making bright and fruitful all the barren spots of earth.
In facing odds and mastering them and rising from defeat,
And making true what once was false, and what was bitter, sweet.
For only he knows perfect joy whose little bit of soil
Is richer ground than what it was when he began to toil

**Anon**

We must accept finite disappointment but we must never lose infinite hope

**Martin Luther King**

For merriment is the birthright of the young. But we can all keep it in our hearts as life goes on if we hold fast by the spirit that refuses to admit defeat; by the faith that never falters, by the hope that cannot be quenched.

**King George VI**

The Spirit guides me here,
To meet upon this hill,
The outstretched arms, the wounded hands,
The love that finds me still.
In silence I am held,
Until my song takes flight
And breaking forth in golden notes
Fills heart and soul with light

When I must leave this place
And face the world again
Good Saviour, from such holy ground
Come with me to the plain.

Consume my soul with fire,
Let love and peace fly free,
And at the end take all I am
And shape what I must be

**Christine McIntosh**
**Cathedral of the Isles, Cumbrae**

God does not die on the day when we cease to believe in a personal deity, but we die on the day when our lives cease to be illumined by the steady radiance, renewed daily, of a wonder, the source of which is beyond all reason

**Dag Hammarskjold**
**Markings**

We shall have to repent in this generation, not so much for the evil deeds of the wicked but for the appalling silence of the good

**Martin Luther King**

God has created me to do Him some definite service; He has committed some work to me which He has not committed to another. I have my mission – I may never know it in this life, but I shall be told it in the next

**Cardinal Newman**
**Meditation**

We are not here to curse the darkness, but to light the candle that can guide us through that darkness to a safe and sane future

**John F. Kennedy**

Don't let me die in the dark, Lord
And not on a winter's day
And not in the afternoon, Lord
When the light is slipping away

But let me go in the morning, Lord
In the sunshine, in the spring

So it won't seem so much like the end, Lord
But the start of everything

**A Prayer**

There is an end to grief
Suddenly there are no more tears to cry
No hurt nor break now
But mute acceptance of what will be
Knowing that each move for good or ill
Must fit the whole
Past comprehension
Yet trusted in the design
This way lies peace

**Brenda Lismer**
**Acceptance**

This piece has given solace to many who are bereaved and seek some consolation in the written word. My thoughts on the subject of 'Acceptance', are further developed in the article I wrote for New Vision, Journal of the Hamblin Trust (see page 70).

> There is nothing in the world of which I feel so certain. I have no idea what it will be like and I am glad that I have not as I am sure it would be wrong. I do not want it for myself as mere continuance but I want it for my understanding of Life. And moreover, 'God is love' appears to me nonsense in view of the world He has made, if there is no other

**William Temple**
**On Eternal Life**

In the Coda to this book, Bishop John Dennis wrote:

> To take the concept of a symphony as a model of the individual's progress through life is imaginative enough. To deal with each of its movements by the quotations in this volume, from sources familiar and less so, is a mark of deep spiritual perception and insight. This is a 'Spiritual Symphony' which strikes deep chords and sympathetic resonances in the mind and heart of the reader.

This book was subsequently published in 2009 by Diadem Books. Our book launch was held at the newly refurbished St. Columba's Retreat House in Woking, in the company of many good friends, the Rt. Rev. John Dennis, former Bishop of St. Edmundsbury and Ipswich, the Very Rev. Alex Wedderspoon, Dean of Guildford Cathedral, and a host of friends – for me, another happy occasion.

'Symphony of Life' is still on sale today, hopefully meeting the needs of all who seek uplift and consolation from the written word.

*   *   *

*Anna signing copies of Symphony of Life*

*Publicity for Words, Music, Stillness*

# Words
# Music
# Stillness

### A time for reflection

12.00 – 13.00 on Mondays

11 January, 1 February, 7 March,
4 April, 9 May, 6 June & 7 July

Coffee will be served from 11.45

at
St. Mary's Church
Quarry St, Guildford

Further details from: anna_jeffery@btinternet.com

## Words
Do you enjoy group discussion?
## Music
Do you value inspirational music?
## Stillness
Are prayer and meditation vital to your spiritual life?

Each session focusses on a word – such as LIFE, ASPIRATION, CHARACTER, COMMITMENT – and on thoughts and writings on that word drawn from the 5 Vision anthologies compiled by Rev. William Sykes, a former Chaplain of University College, Oxford. He compiled the anthologies as part of a quest to rediscover his faith.

Words Music Stillness offers us the opportunity to explore, renew and enlarge our faith.

Inspiring music and stillness conclude the hour.

All are welcome.

# V

# WORDS, MUSIC, STILLNESS

Some years ago, browsing in the Guildford cathedral bookshop, I came across a quite superb anthology – or rather five anthologies – written by the Chaplain of University College, Oxford, William Sykes. At the age of thirty, having just completed a busy four-year curacy at Bradford Cathedral, William was aware of being, as he put it, 'spiritually bankrupt'. Subsequently he embarked on a quest to find and restore what had been lost. He attempted to study the writings of mankind.

The result of this search was the publication of his five anthologies:

> VISIONS OF FAITH
> VISIONS OF HOPE
> VISIONS OF LOVE
> VISIONS OF GRACE
> VISIONS OF GLORY

To this he subsequently added: THE ETERNAL VISION.

Each volume included the spiritual experiences and insights of poets, playwrights, ordained men and women, novelists, philosophers, scientists, historians, politicians, economists, psychologists, statesmen, artists and musicians. William then conceived the idea of using this material as a source for reflection/discussion amongst undergraduates and graduates at Oxford who were interested in participating. These 'Reflection Groups' became hugely successful and an important part of university life for many. As one participant has said:

> These anthologies are just so much more than mere quotations from the bible. I've read all of William's anthologies and have copied the best quotations to take with me everywhere. I buy the books regularly for my friends and family as I believe that thinking about matters beyond our day to day life can help us be more grounded and content. I look up 'friendship' after a row with a friend or 'loneliness' when I feel lonely. The chapter on

'Awareness' helped me get to know myself better and the whole book made me realise what is really important in life.

Within these five anthologies, one finds a breadth of concern for the fears and obstacles as well as the triumphs and quiet satisfactions, that we all face. The readings are drawn not just from the Christian testaments and canons but also from a wide field of saints and more than a few sinners. They are prefaced in each topic by one of William's encounters with the problem enshrined by the heading. Within these writings, William has grappled with our demons but he has also seen our strengths. We should not be distracted by his sharing of his battles with doubt and fear. He shares as much of his wonder at grace and faith. He truly was a remarkable man.

Soon after discovering these volumes, I had an opportunity to meet William in Oxford. Tentatively I asked him if he would give his blessing to the idea that I too should set up a similar group in Guildford – and to my immense delight, he wholeheartedly gave it, urging me to 'quietly get on with it' with unconditional access to his source material.

And so it was that some years later, the time seemed right to form a group in Guildford – under the name of **'Words, Music and Stillness'** – using William's concept of selecting one word from his anthologies for discussion, each time the group met. In addition I added the concept of classical music and a period of stillness – to make up the hour over mid-day. This modification on William's original concept of Reflection has added a new dimension to many people's lives and has become a valuable form of ministry in the local community. However, this project – I must hasten to add – would not have come to fruition without my husband's brilliant assistance as Group Facilitator!

With the help of the team at St. Mary's Church, Guildford, we launched the concept in March 2015 and the group still thrives today.

Here is a sample of some of the material and music we have used in the group over the past year:

## **GUIDANCE**

Let me think that there is one among those stars that guides my life through the dark unknown
**Rabindranath Tagore, Stray Birds**

We are not meant to live solely by intellectual convictions, we are meant more and more to open ourselves to the Spirit
**Basil Hume OSB, Searching for God**

God shall be my hope,
My stay, my guide, and lantern to my feet
**William Shakespeare, King Henry VI**

There is a spirit that works within us, and develops a power in us that teaches us how to accomplish what we will and guides us by its inspiration to successful results
**Henry Ward Beecher, Proverbs from Plymouth Pulpit**

Guidance does not end when calamity begins. In every situation He meets us and out of every situation He can lead us to a greener pasture and a sphere of wider use.
**W.E.Sangster, God Does Guide Us**

We do not need to be very old to look back on life and see that things that we thought were disasters worked out to our good; things that we thought were disappointments worked out to greater blessings. We can look back and we can see a guiding and a directing hand in it and through it all
**William Barclay, The Letter to the Romans**

## CONTENTMENT

We only see in a lifetime a dozen faces marked with the peace of a contented spirit
**Henry Ward Beecher, Proverbs from Plymouth Pulpit**

To be content with little is difficult; to be content with much, impossible
**Old proverb**

Content and discontent should run in and out of each other in every true man's life. Every man should have a generous discontent with what he has attained and strive to go upwards
**Henry Ward Beecher, Proverbs from Plymouth Pulpit**

Let us be contented with what has happened to us and thankful for all we have been spared. Let us accept the natural order in which we move. Let us reconcile ourselves to the mysterious rhythm of our destinies, such as they

must be in this world of space and time. Let us treasure our joys but not bewail our sorrows. The glory of light cannot exist without its shadows.
**William S. Churchill, Thoughts and Adventures**


## ACCEPTANCE

We must accept finite disappointment but we must never lose infinite hope
**Martin Luther King**

The will of God... cannot be simply that we accept the situations of life but must be rather that we go through them and emerge from them
**John S. Dunne, The Reasons of the Heart**

You often try to run away from your life but you are wasting your time. If you sincerely believe that your life is worthwhile and necessary, then you will have accepted it
**Michel Quoist, With Open Heart**

Items of music that we have used in the group include:

*Parry: I was glad*

*Rutter: The Lord bless you and keep you*

*Mozart: Ave verum corpus*

*Johann Sebastian Bach: Suite No.3 in D major*

*Berlioz: Sanctus from his Te Deum*

*Karl Jenkins, Benedictus, from The Armed Man: A Mass for Peace*

Following the music and the closing minutes of stillness, prayer and contemplation, the whole provides a sanctuary from the stress and busyness of life today – all within the serene beauty of St. Mary's church, Guildford.

\* \* \*

# VI

# A CATHEDRAL DREAM

Over the years, I have had ideas for various projects – some have come to fruition – some not.

This one is very much on the 'back burner' as it were, waiting for the right moment to take it further...

---

WHAT IS THIS DREAM?

The establishment of a new, non-resident, Lay Community of the Holy Spirit at Guildford Cathedral

WHY?

Having been members of other lay communities in the past, (I was an Associate of St. Peter's, Woking (adjacent to St. Columba's House) until the mother house was sold and the few surviving members dispersed to nursing homes in and around the area. I have enjoyed many conversations with Mother Rosamund during this time when Reverend Mother had expressed her wish that the Community should have closer links with the cathedral in the future. Sadly she was admitted to a nursing home before this hope could materialise. Thus the vision came to me that a new lay community might be established with its base at the cathedral.

Michael, my husband, has belonged to the Fellowship of St. John for many years. Both Communities are now disbanded. Both offered valuable fellowship and a discipline which enhanced our spiritual lives in a way not available through local churches

WHY NOT BECOME FRANCISCAN TERTIARIES?

No comparable teaching available as would be at the cathedral with its team – Dean, Sub-Dean, Residentiary and Honorary Canons.

No mother house as there is at the cathedral.

No strong musical tradition as at the cathedral.

HOW WOULD SUCH A CONCEPT WORK?

Initially through application and formal acceptance at the cathedral.

Through the establishment of a Rule.

Through prescribed times set aside each day for prayer, reflection and spiritual reading.

Through offering voluntary work and or other gifts for the benefit of the cathedral.

Through regular and committed attendance at Cathedral Services.

WHAT WOULD IT GIVE THE CATHEDRAL?

A core community whose skills could be drawn on as appropriate. It would represent a new concept in cathedral commitment which could well be taken up nationwide.

Financial support to the cathedral by legacies/lump sums as offered by new postulants entering convents and other communities.

WHAT WOULD IT GIVE TO MEMBERS OF SUCH A COMMUNITY NOT ALREADY AVAILABLE TO MEMBERS OF THE CATHEDRAL CONGREGATION?

A more structured spiritual life not possible with mere church attendance.

A tighter knit community because of the Vows they would take.

A more disciplined community because of the structure in the Rule.

Opportunity for disciplined teaching (i.e. retreats, study days etc.)

WHO WOULD LEAD IT?

Under the broad wing of the Dean but a staff member of the cathedral, one of the Canons or Honorary Canons perhaps or even someone with a special interest from outside the cathedral, might lead its day to day activities.

PROPOSED NUMBER THAT MIGHT MAKE UP SUCH A COMMUNITY

Small core group initially – between 6 and 20.

(former Dean, Alex Wedderspoon, named several whom he was certain would support it and form such a core group)

THOSE WHO HAVE INDICATED SUPPORT OF SUCH A CONCEPT

Former Dean, Very Rev. Alex Wedderspoon

Rt. Rev. John Dennis, Winchester, (former Bishop of St. Edmundsbury & Ipswich)

Rev. Barry Preece (formerly priest at the Clandon churches and Diocesan Adviser in Spirituality – now retired)

Canon Nick Whitehead, Shere

Canon Alan Hargrave – Ely Cathedral

Father Jeffries, Roman Catholic Priest at St. Cuthman's, Coolham

WHY AT THE CATHEDRAL AND NOT ANY OF THE PARISH CHURCHES IN THE DIOCESE?

The cathedral has a huge standing in the diocese with centuries old tradition of glorious sacred music and scholarship; the standard of teaching and preaching second to none with all the attendant facilities that come with the cathedral (i.e. Education Centre, Library etc.)

The fact that many of our cathedrals started life as monasteries initially adds weight to this natural development of cathedral life

**AJ**
**Spring 2012**

# SECTION IV

Articles Written for New Vision Magazine
(Journal of the Hamblin Trust)

I: Spring 2014: Heart Of The Matter

II: Winter 2014: Acceptance

III: Spring 2015: Trilogy On Truth

IV: Winter 2015: Essential Connections

V: Summer 2016:
Held In Perfect Balance: Being & Doing

# I

# ARTICLES WRITTEN FOR 'NEW VISION' THE MAGAZINE OF THE HAMBLIN TRUST

Some years ago, while working as a volunteer at The Harry Edwards Healing Sanctuary, I came across a copy of New Vision – the magazine of The Hamblin Trust – and was so impressed with its quality and content – I contacted the office and took out a subscription immediately.

A little while later – through various opportunities for contact with the Editor, I was invited to write an article for the journal – and over the years, have continued writing for them from time to time. It is a privilege and a joy to do so – and five of these articles appear in this section. They cover my own 'credo' and some of its components – thoughts on accepting where we are, the 'truth' at its heart and relationships essential to it. Also some thoughts on how to hold the balance between faith and works, Mary and Martha, being and doing...

# II

## THE HEART OF THE MATTER: A PERSONAL CREDO
### by Anna Jeffery

'He who knows others is wise;
he who knows himself is enlightened.'
Lao Tzu

To know ourselves and to formulate our own philosophy of life, is surely essential as we journey in pilgrimage through this life. How else will we find The Way if no goals or values are set? A structured belief system, a personal philosophy, a valid credo, saves us from:

> A life without meaning
> A life without values
> A life without hope

Thus we will have

> A purpose to live for
> A self to live with
> A faith to live by

I believe – as do many spiritual gurus, that we are spiritual beings on a human journey rather than human beings on a spiritual journey. We are pilgrims and as pilgrims, we seek meaning, healing, religious insights and affirmations. Our chosen sacred destination is the gateway for a life changing experience. We have a focus and attention that is different from a tourist. We seek answers to ultimate questions. As pilgrims, we remove the constraints of ordinary life so that we experience the mysterious and the miraculous. Through meditation and prayer we unburden our minds, seek healing, give thanks and renew our faith. Rewards come just as much from the journey as the destination.

In this game of life, there are several ways to win. What we choose for the end goal is up to each of us – many choose to focus on fulfilling their life calling and purpose. That life choice will impact every area of our lives. Each of us has hidden gifts, untapped talents and undeveloped skills – these define our potential and discovering our potential – the potential known only to God – can change our lives.

I believe that here on earth through the joys and heartbreaks of each character-building event or experience, we are given the opportunity to become the kind of person God alone knows we have the potential to become. For those who live without an idea of their life-calling, life purpose and potential, it is like walking through a strange forest without a compass. Life becomes a series of problems, setbacks, heartbreaks and disappointments. For most of us, these life lessons only make sense in the light of our life-calling and purpose.

Our life calling is what we are to give to the world. What we are called to do and become;

Our life purpose is why we are here, the lessons, experience and understanding we take with us when we leave this world.

I believe that during this journey called Life, a journey towards God, we meet with very significant people who draw alongside us for a period, helping us to a 'closer walk with God'. My own life has been punctuated by meetings with such people – some have been with me briefly, others for the duration. Our guardian angel also accompanies us on this journey.

I believe that in solitude and silence, we find that essential life-giving succour to be found only when we draw apart:

Our external environment is so busy, so full of stimulation, it is a real challenge to take ourselves away long enough to take a good look inside: we need to stop, unplug, and Just Be! Self-exploration involves looking hard at our thoughts, feelings, behaviour, motivations – looking at the roots of who we are and the standards and values that shape our lives.

> Many people today look for silence, solitude and peace. They dream of places where they can rest away from the daily hassle of living which tear them apart, exhaust them and leave them dissatisfied, wounded and bleeding and always alone. But they won't necessarily find peace and quiet waiting for them in other places. There is a place within us where quiet reigns – the centre, our heart of hearts. There we can find him who is the plenitude of silence. But who will guide us there? We must learn the way.

(Michael Quoist – With Open Heart – translated by Colette Copeland (Gill and Macmillan, 1983)

Anna Jeffery

**(First published in the Spring 2014 edition of New Vision, Journal of the Hamblin Trust, and reprinted by kind permission of the Editor)**

# III

# ACCEPTANCE
by Anna Jeffery

**This Way Lies Peace**

There is an end to grief
Suddenly there are no more tears to cry
No hurt nor break now
But mute acceptance of what will be
Knowing that each move for good or ill
Must fit the whole
Past comprehension
Yet trusted in the design
This way lies peace

**Brenda Lismer**

There are times when a piece of writing brings us to our knees in gratitude for expressing what we cannot – these hauntingly beautiful words from Brenda Lismer give timeless yet magisterial comfort so that however devastating the grief – the life-changing diagnosis – the cruel twist of fate, the missed opportunity, we are able to bear it. She sees with an inner eye and knows with an intuitive certainty that there is an over-arching Mind that is Love.

As we travel through life and come up against events that would break us, we need to look beyond them to see the lessons that will make us – so that we become stronger, more triumphant human beings

With this understanding, there is no need to ask

Why me?
Why this?
Why now?

However, Acceptance is one of the hardest gates to pass through – they stand proud far along the road ahead but demons block the way – demons of fear, anger, resentment, anxiety, so that reaching the summer lands ahead, is never easy. It takes more than courage to pass through these gates – it takes blind faith and trust – to reach the mute acceptance of which Brenda Lismer speaks.

We need therefore to look at these life-changing events with a positive mindset. Instead of a negative and defeatist attitude we must realise that acceptance is the key with which we move from life-changing sadness to new horizons and transcendence and thus enduring happiness. The lesson or purpose behind every challenge will help us to embrace it – accept it – instead of resisting, believing that everything happens for a reason.

But we do not need to understand that reason or understand why something has happened – our understanding can wait – our acceptance cannot. So instead of complaining and over-dwelling on it, we need to choose to live with it – to live because of it. And instead of staring at the closed door in front of us, let us turn our back on it and see how many windows are open all around us.

As Arthur Rubinstein advocates – we should develop 'an unconditional acceptance of life and what it brings'.

The reason for what happens in our lives, all that we do, the meaning of it, is incomprehensible and will probably remain so, at least during this life. Instead we must face change or disaster in the most creative way possible. 'We must accept disappointment and change but we must never lose hope' urges Martin Luther King.

And so with this new understanding and discernment, we return to our key passage:

> .....knowing that each move for good or ill
> Must fit the whole
> Past comprehension
> Yet trusted in the design
> This way lies peace.

Anna Jeffery

**(First published in the Winter 2014 edition of New Vision, Journal of the Hamblin Trust and reprinted by kind permission of the Editor)**

# IV

## A TRILOGY ON TRUTH
### by Anna Jeffery

A vast amount has been written about Truth over the years – three of my favourites are pieces by Reuel L. Howe, J. Neville Ward and William Barclay.

First, this short piece by Reuel L. Howe:

**The purpose of obedience to truth is not to graze in the flat lands but to climb the sharp, high, narrow ridges of faith in order that we may understand more and more the relevance of the revelation of God to our own age.**

*Reuel L. Howe, The Miracle of Dialogue, The Saint Andrew Press, 1969, p.125

If we merely free-wheeled through life, avoiding challenges, hardships, dangers or disasters, then how would we experience the life-giving elixir that is Truth? Our legacy would be as a stone, rough-hewn and unfinished, rather than the polished work of perfection we could be. We must, therefore, find the courage to tackle life's challenges head on – in faith – with the shield of Truth before us, so that we are free to reach for the brightest and best that we can be.

Secondly, this by J. Neville Ward:

**There is truth that merely brightens and intrigues the mind for a while and truth which we are able to take deeply into ourselves to help us make a more constructive response to our challenges and anxieties.**

** J.Neville Ward, Friday Afternoon, Epworth Press, 1989, p.118

Here the writer focuses on what he calls; 'the truth that brightens ...' ie.

'If you tell the truth, you don't have to remember anything'
or
'The truth doesn't cost anything but a lie could cost you everything'

However, we must focus on the more profound, enduring truths by which to live and work through challenges and anxieties. Here lies the battle cry to muster all the inner strength and resources available when we are truly up against the worst that life can throw at us – sudden bereavement – physical terror – cataclysmic flood or storm – and other traumas of this mortal life. Now indeed more than ever comes the need to hold on and endure, with all that we have known of Truth, Faith and Courage to sustain us.

And to close our trilogy, this from William Barclay who writes in his typically simple yet profound style:

**...the truth which Jesus brings to us shows us the real values of life. The fundamental question to which every man has to give an answer is: 'To what am I to give my life? Am I to give it to a career? Am I to give it to the amassing of material possessions? Am I to give it to pleasure? Am I to give it to the obedience and to the service of God?' The truth which Jesus brings enables us to get our scale of values right; it is in His truth that we see what things are really important and what things are not.**

\*\*\* William Barclay, The Gospel of John, The Saint Andrew Press, 1965, vol. 2, page 25

He gets quickly to the heart of the matter and what lies at the heart of life. Young souls may go blithely on, sewing their wild oats in total disregard of a deeper, more enduring purpose. Wiser, more mature souls however, sense the significance of making the most of opportunities to develop their spiritual lives, to give something that will enrich both their own and the lives of all with whom they come into contact, never easy and always challenging in this secular world that eschews principles, high values and all that would contribute to spiritual maturity.

The preference very often is for the secular life, heads down – wasting and squandering – instead of looking upwards and within to the wealth of spiritual riches and life deepening experiences – the hallmark choice of those who follow the Truth: 'I am the way, the truth and the life' and 'The Truth shall set you free' is the counsel from the highest authority – we ignore it at our peril.

Finally, let Alistair MacLean have the last word:

**'Truth is whatever cleanses you and delights the higher you in you. Truth is whatever summons your spirit to do battle in her service. Truth is whatever makes you or me, one with the mind of God'**

\*\*\*\* Alistair MacLean, The Happy Finder, Allenson & Co. 1949 p.71

Anna Jeffery

(Inspired and written during a performance of Bach's Mass in B Minor, Guildford Cathedral, November 2014)

**(First published in the Spring 2015 edition of New Vision, Journal of the Hamblin Trust and reprinted by kind permission of the Editor)**

# V

## ESSENTIAL CONNECTIONS
By Anna Jeffery

I have always enjoyed reflecting on the wise words of great men and women. Unfailingly they give me a sense of perspective and never fail to inspire. I know that many of you will feel the same. In this short article, I would like to share with you the inspiring words of Swedish diplomat, economist and author, Dag Hammarskjold (1905-1961), poet par excellence, John Donne (1572-1631) and that giant among men, Martin Luther King (1929-1968).

INNER CONNECTIONS: A LIFE OF STILLNESS

**'God does not die on the day when we cease to believe in a personal deity but we die on the day when our lives cease to be illumined by the steady radiance, renewed daily, of a wonder, the source of which is beyond all reason'**

Dag Hammarskjold, Markings

Indeed this wonder should never cease to be an inspirational source – and we should especially value an inner life which can be a sea of glass, a life of perfect, essential composure – a great calm – there if we seek it. And part of the discipline of the spiritual life is designed to bring the insights and the inspiration of this stillness from our inner lives to bear on our outer lives – in our relationships with our fellows and through our responsibilities towards family and the wider community.

We had the privilege of knowing and serving under a former Dean of Guildford Cathedral who emanated such stillness and deep spirituality – now sorely missed since his death some months ago.

OUTER CONNECTIONS: LIVING WITH OTHERS

**No man is an island entire of itself; every man
is a piece of the continent, a part of the main;**

John Donne's masterpiece: 'No man is an Island' – beautifully illustrates that however rich our inner lives, the richness is lost if we fail to let this inner light shine out. All human beings are connected but if we become isolated from others, we do not thrive – our light does not shine. Living in isolation is a calling for only the few.

Donne feels that all mankind is one – each person's existence affects the existence of another and in the great cycle of life and death, although we must ultimately die, we are all important as members of the human race and our very existence makes its own contribution to mankind, however insignificant and useless we may feel. Through this well known work, Donne brings us a message of hope and an understanding of the meaning of our lives. As the British actress Gina Bellman puts it:

**'I love those connections that make this big old world feel like a little village'**

It seems to me that relationships create psychological space and safety so that we can explore and learn ¬ and being part of something bigger than ourselves – (church membership, voluntary work, teaching, and other similar institutions), gives meaning and focus to our lives. We are energised by living with, through and for – others – as in a crisis of an international or personal nature, such a group dynamic enables us to grow. The phrases in Donne's poem have forever connected men with each other, proving that all human beings are inter-related and stressing that throughout life, human relationships have a value which is immeasurable.

ULTIMATE CONNECTIONS: IN TOUCH WITH THE DIVINE

**'Seek God and discover Him and make Him a power in your life. Without Him, all our efforts turn to ashes and our sunrises into darker nights. Without Him, life is a meaningless drama with the decisive scenes missing. But with Him, we are able to rise from the fatigue of despair to the buoyancy of hope. With Him we are able to rise from the midnight of desperation to the daybreak of joy. St. Augustine was right – we were made for God and we will be restless until we find our rest in Him'**

Martin Luther King
The Words of Martin Luther King

Martin Luther King writes eloquently of the value of our relationship with God – however tenuous and faltering our search – nevertheless the underlying order and meaning of life is ultimately revealed and the eternal harmony shines through. God's divine wisdom and purpose which is completely beyond our comprehension, is there – we just need to make the connection.

Anna Jeffery

**(First published in the Winter 2015 edition of New Vision, the Journal of the Hamblin Trust and reprinted by kind permission of the Editor)**

# VI

## HELD IN PERFECT BALANCE
by Anna Jeffery

I have been thinking lately about the idea of Being versus Doing – the concept that we get so caught up in things we have to do that we stop simply Being, stop growing and stop developing as human beings. Yes, we take in more information, and we learn more ways to do things but what do we learn about who we are and how we fit in on this planet? What do we learn about our relationship to God and life and love and how do we grow as the spiritual beings that we are?

I think we get caught in this dilemma because Doing is so much easier – we can quantify what we do – the results are there to see and count and judge. Not so with Being. But there has to be time for Being – in fact this is an essential part of our human journey as spiritual beings – to explore and learn in earth's classroom. In this we are drawn to connect with the Divine because seeking higher knowledge is associated with Being – the need to establish islands of calm in life's turbulent seas and give ourselves permission to simply do nothing at all.

Being is getting in touch with that deeper part of ourselves, the inner power that many call 'spirit' others call 'God' the part of me that can help define who I am in this world, as opposed to what I do. We are here on earth to live, experience things and learn – which means 'to be.' Yet at the same time, we need to survive in the physical realm (i.e. working, earning a living or 'doing.') After all, we do exist in a physical reality. There are things we need to 'do' in order to reach our physical and spiritual goals. But trying to balance the spiritual and the material is like being on a see-saw with one side 'being' and the other 'doing.' Ideally we should have enough 'being' time and enough 'doing' time to feel balanced. Finding that balance is an essential challenge of being human but finding time to nurture both is not easy. Time for prayer and reflection is hard to come by yet is essential to retain our spiritual sanity. People who work and minister without adequate restoration through prayer and meditation, do not have the interior resources to cope with what life throws at them or to manifest the fruits of the Spirit in a stress-filled world. It is during the quiet times of the devotional life that we gain the perspective and power we need to live with character and composure in the context of daily demands.

And so perfect balance requires a rhythm of the kind shown below:

solitude................engagement
interior.................exterior
invisible...............visible
reflective life .......real life
rest ......................work
restoration of spiritual energy; application of spiritual energy

The Being life of the left column should energise the Doing life of the right. Our aim as spiritual beings on a human journey, should be to keep closely in touch with our spiritual source so that we are totally balanced in all that we do and are.

Have you ever met someone who is calm and peaceful, loving and caring? They seem to have a radiance that the rest of us would love to have as a result of their being able to get in touch with who they are rather than what they do. I have been privileged to meet several such people during my lifetime, each of whom radiate this shining inner spirit – truly I can say I have seen glimpses of heaven through them and within them. Their focus on Being and Doing has been maintained in perfect balance.

However, we must not so immerse ourselves in spirituality that it becomes an escape and we are 'too heavenly minded to be of any earthly use.' Forsaking the human world and forcing ourselves to live on an ethereal plane we become ungrounded. The key is balance in all things. We are so much more than our jobs and our roles in society, we are essentially spiritual beings with sparks of divine consciousness. We need to take the time to recognize that within ourselves and others.

O gift of God! A perfect day,
whereon shall no man
work but play,
whereon it is enough for me
not to be (always) doing but to be

Henry Wordsworth Longfellow
1807-1882

Anna Jeffery

**(First published in the Summer 2016 edition of New Vision, Journal of the Hamblin Trust and reprinted by kind permission of the Editor)**

# SECTION V

## Significant Places

Part I: St. Cuthman's

Part II: St. Columba's House and Associate Years

Part III: Cathedral Of The Isles, Cumbrae

Part IV: Portmeirion

Part V: Harry Edwards Healing Sanctuary

Part VI: Orchard Cottage

# I

## ST. CUTHMAN'S RETREAT HOUSE

I first came upon St. Cuthman's – known originally as St. Julian's – in my London days when this very special retreat house, deep in the heart of Sussex, proved such a haven of rest, a welcome retreat from the noise, pollution and distraction of all that London was. I so needed the balm and comfort that wrapped around one upon stepping inside such a gracious building with its roaring log fires in winter and the beauty of the lake and grounds all around.

In those early days, it was run by a small lay community established originally by Florence Allshorn, a member of the Church Missionary Society, who trained students for service abroad. She had a particular dream for her students when they returned from abroad: '...a dream of a house in some lovely secluded place where you could come and be quiet and rest, read and talk.' Thus it was that her dedication, vision and commitment led to the purchase in 1950 of a property where the missionary community could find essential rest and peace, 'take in beauty' with superb paintings, antiques, splendid grounds and reflective space – thus finding strength to return overseas, rested, re-charged and re-invigorated. St. Julian's flourished and became an important and much loved place in the lives of many people.

Eventually however, the community became too frail and too few in number to continue. The house was sold on to the Roman Catholic Diocese of Arundel and Brighton who continued the work started all those years ago by Florence Allshorn. Today, with a new name, (formerly St. Julians, now St. Cuthman's) and much skilled modernisation of its facilities, it retains the unique character of the house. It is well used as a retreat house and conference centre, providing rest, renewal and peace for all who come.

The house is set within twenty-five acres of fields and woodland with access to the South Downs and the historic Sussex countryside. It has an excellent library with resources constantly being renewed.

The small Chapel is separate from the house with a wonderful view of the grounds beyond the altar window. The chapel has been a place of worship since 1944 and daily services continue today. The new window at the entrance to the chapel is inscribed with the words of the poet George Herbert: 'Love Bade me Welcome'. This, in essence, is what St. Cuthman's is about.

The house has, over forty years, been for me a place of immense significance and with visits twice a year, represents a place of prayer where life-changing decisions have been made. Always refreshing. Always humbling. Always meeting a need. A truly joyous place.

*** 

*St. Cuthman's Retreat House, Coolham*

# II

# ST. COLUMBA'S RETREAT HOUSE

This represents a rather more local 'sanctuary' or place of escape for much needed peace and quiet with its opportunities for prayer and study – another lifeline – when the world and its busyness threatens to overwhelm.

Saint Columba's House is owned and managed by the Trustees of Saint Peter's Home and Sisterhood. The Community of St. Peter was founded in 1861 as a nursing order of Anglican nuns.

Circumstances took me there some years ago for retreats and Quiet Days and it was during these that I had many enriching and meaningful conversations with the Sisters. This eventually led to my being formally accepted as an Associate member of the Community – an immense privilege. I remember Mother Superior saying, on the day of my Acceptance in their simple chapel, 'Come as often as you can, Anna – this is your home.'

Sadly, years later as the Sisters aged and became too frail even to run the smaller, purpose-built house in the grounds of the retreat house, places were found for them in care homes and private houses around the country, and all resources became centred on the main building and its adjoining Redwood House. The whole was upgraded and superbly refurbished to meet the needs of today. Thus St. Columba's House was re-opened in the early years of the new millennium to provide hospitality, conference facilities and offer a spirituality programme drawing on a variety of Christian traditions. The Mother Superior of the Community of Saint Peter remains in the Woking area.

With vivid memories of my time as an Associate of St. Peter's and the warmth and care of the Sisters, St. Columba's House represents a precious space – a place of meaning – with memories, especially of the launch of my second book, 'Symphony of Life', early in January 2010.

\* \* \*

# III

# CATHEDRAL OF THE ISLES, CUMBRAE

Looking through the annual programme of Retreats, published by the National Retreat Association many years ago, I happened to come across details of a retreat house, The College of the Holy Spirit, centred on The Isle of Cumbrae. And so it was, a few months later, Michael and I were on a train to Scotland.

The College is part guest-house and part Christian retreat house located next to the UK's smallest cathedral, the Cathedral of The Isles. Both were built at the same time in 1851 by the architect William Butterfield. The College was originally built for students of theology in the Scottish Episcopal Church. The aim of the College of the Holy Spirit (with the Cathedral) is to create a centre for spiritual development and artistic expression for individuals and groups, and to offer hospitality to guests as well as the local community on the Isle of Cumbrae.

We fell in love with the place immediately. The island is a walkers' paradise with views stretching far and wide to adjoining islands and beyond, and, wherever one goes, one is conscious of the deep spiritual tradition associated with this centre of spirituality.

I am always deeply moved whenever I read and re-read two poems written for Cumbrae by Christine McIntosh, a local poet:

The first – Hymn for Cumbrae:

The Spirit guides me here,
to meet upon this hill
The outstretched arms, the wounded hands,
The love that finds me still.

In silence I am held,
Until my song takes flight
and breaking forth in golden notes
Fills heart and soul with light.

When I must leave this place
And face the world again
Good Saviour, from such holy ground
Come with me to the plain.

Consume my soul with fire,
Let love and peace fly free,
And at the end take all I am
And shape what I must be.

(There was a particularly moving occasion when we sang this to the familiar hymn tune 'Blest are the pure in heart' during Morning Service in the Cathedral here)

And the second poem:

There was a church, rising
Above green terraces of
Pleasing symmetry,
Surely too neat, too
Small to encompass much
Mystery.

Yet in that
Silent shell, in the golden
Brass-glow of candles,
God would touch
Careless souls, catch their
Hearts in a mesh of
Incandescent song, so that
Those who knelt there would
Pass through the veil of light
To the bright places beyond.

Both of these put beautifully into words the emotions and a deep love for the place that only a gifted poet can do.

We return to the Island as often as we can.

\* \* \*

# IV

# PORTMEIRION

We discovered Portmeirion – an absolute gem – a delight – a place of wondrous beauty – far back in the 1990s, soon after a fire had ravaged the hotel.

The village is located in the community of Penrhyndeudraeth, on the estuary of the River Dwyrd, two miles south east of Porthmadog and consists of the main hotel with a superb coastal position overlooking the estuary.

From the advertisement, it sounded to me an ideal holiday venue for my architect husband, as it had been built and designed by the well-known architect Sir Clough Williams-Ellis between 1925 and 1975, in the style of an Italian village and is now owned by a charitable trust.

Sir Clough Williams-Ellis, an architect and Portmeirion's designer, built the village as a 'fantasy'- or as Lewis Mumford wrote of it in his book 'The Highway and the City':

> Portmeirion is an artful and playful little modern village, designed as a whole and all of a piece... a fantastic collection of architectural relics and impish modern fantasies. In a sense, Portmeirion is a deliberately irresponsible reaction against the dull sterilities of so much that passes as modern architecture today...

The village itself has always been run as a hotel using the majority of the buildings as hotel rooms or self-catering cottages, together with shops, a cafe, tea-room and restaurant. It is utterly beautiful, enchanting with the charm and elegance of a bygone age. Newcomers almost always fall under its spell – to return again and again.

We have enjoyed many self-catering family holidays there especially in The Dolphin, Government House and other cottages around the village, all of which have superb facilities, with easy access to the peninsula and its thickly growing rhododendrons and other lush vegetation flourishing in the temperate climate.

The estuary with its stunning views across the bay, is a place of peace and inspiration, especially in the evening, when the day visitors have left, as quoted below in a local leaflet:

> In the evening, after the day trippers have gone, a deep tranquillity settles over the village. One by one lights come on in the cottages, residents stroll about in the gentle air and a sense of enchantment is everywhere.
> **Australian Gourmet**

> That night, when we reached our suite, its wide windows revealed a scene of ephemeral splendour. The sea's silent invasion of the estuary was complete. The tide had flooded the sand. A full moon silvered the water. Beyond, dark mounded hills bore clusters of lights like earthbound stars.
> **The Washington Post**

This indeed says it all – and our family return again and again whenever we can – for birthdays, celebrations and indeed just for the sheer pleasure of the place.

\* \* \*

*The bay at Portmeirion*

PORTMEIRION

# V

# HARRY EDWARDS HEALING SANCTUARY

Having retired in the Spring of 2009, I found myself with time on my hands that summer and so began exploring possibilities in the voluntary sector.

And thus it was, one morning during Autumn 2009, I made my way over to Shere where volunteers were being sought at the Harry Edwards Healing Sanctuary. The Sanctuary is nestled in thirty acres of Surrey woodland at Burrows Lea, just outside the village. It was founded in 1946 by the world renowned spiritual healer Harry Edwards and soon became an internationally recognised healing centre.

As my car swung through the entrance, a landscape of stunning beauty lay before me and I felt captivated. The thirty or so acres of grounds were cultivated rather than manicured, with acres and acres of lush shrubbery, trees, green spaces and unparalleled distant views across the Surrey hills. Closer to the house itself, gardens had been tended lovingly with lily ponds, goldfish, cut hedges, freshly mown lawns – an unimaginable oasis of calm.

Within the house itself were soft furnishings, subtle lighting, treatment rooms, the chapel, dining room and well appointed office space, with six beautifully furnished bedrooms for Retreat guests.

Soon after my appointment as a volunteer, I was thrilled to be offered a key administrative role, organising the Sanctuary's fund-raising fairs (three each year: a Spring Fair, a Summer Open Day and an Autumn Fair) – a demanding role, involving a high level of detailed planning, organisation, budgetary considerations and liaison with a range of people within and outside the Sanctuary. In addition, I was also invited to organise their annual Carol Service, no small task and this again involved detailed liaison and co-ordination with a wide range of people, including the two local Junior Schools (Shere Infants and Peaslake Infants whose older children would feature prominently in the Service), inviting the local vicar to direct the Service, appointing an organist, arranging for one of the healers to act as Father Christmas and present gifts to the children, printing the Service Sheet, invitations to the guests, parents and staff, all the details involved in an event of this kind. I licked my lips in anticipation of getting to grips with these new challenges.

Then followed six very happy years working in this inspirational place.

But returning to my theme of 'the golden thread running through our lives if we will only follow it', one day, while in the well stocked library at the Sanctuary, I picked up a copy of a journal entitled 'New Vision' published by the Hamblin Trust, Bosham – and loved it straightaway. The articles were largely based on spiritual themes by a range of writers – all stimulating, absorbing and I immediately wrote and arranged a subscription. It was several months later that, having been in touch with the Editor, I was invited to write articles for the journal, on a range of topics – Truth – Awareness – Acceptance – Being and Doing.

But yet another extraordinary happening occurred while I was working at the Sanctuary – I found a separate printed sheet in another copy of New Vision, detailing the work at Fintry, a retreat house with a small resident community on the outskirts of Milford, Surrey, and some years later, formed a lasting friendship resulting in valuable spiritual guidance, with one of the senior members of this Community (see p.114).

So many images, impressions, valuable contacts, coincidences, and much happiness followed my appointment as a volunteer at the Sanctuary, but eventually the golden thread was leading me to new challenges, new beginnings, and so I moved on.

\* \* \*

# HEALING AND THE SANCTUARY

For over 60 years we have helped many thousands of people to ease their aches, pains, stress and all kinds of illness

Tel: 01483 202054
Email: healing@burrowslea.org.uk
www.sanctuary-burrowslea.org.uk

HARRY EDWARDS
**healingsanctuary**

Registered Charity Number 1098712

# VI

# ORCHARD COTTAGE

I could hardly write about 'significant places' without reference to the most significant of places for me – Orchard Cottage – our home, tucked away on land adjacent to the Common, just outside Guildford. The cottage is an elm-board gabled building with elements of the 1920s Arts and Crafts style, situated in three quarters of an acre of ground, with spreading lawns, fruit trees, brick paths, roses around the door, pleasing vistas everywhere.

Orchard Cottage can only be described as a joy – a little piece of paradise. Built in 1921 by my husband's great uncle, it has remained in the family to this day. It was a place my husband knew and loved from his earliest years, a dream realised in 1981 when we purchased the cottage from his aunt – or 'Aunty Marjorie' as she was always known – and it has been our home for the last 35 years.

It is to Aunty Marjorie that I owe my name! My husband's former wife had the same Christian name as my own (Shirley), and upon first meeting me, she said firmly, 'I will call you Anna!' And that is who I am - and have been, to this day!

Aunty Marjorie imbued the cottage with a sense of calm and wellbeing, as she herself embraced graciousness and wisdom, enhancing the lives of all who met her. Enormously respected by the family, I so enjoyed the times we sat together, exchanging views and putting the world to rights. We shared aspects of the spiritual dimension, though her beliefs were drawn more from Eastern sources rather than traditional Anglican views. Marrying later in life, she had found love with a distant admirer who asked one day if he could set up his easel and paint the cottage. The rest is history!

But a cruel twist of fate brought his untimely death after only eight or so years together, while simultaneously Aunty Marjorie struggled with the burden of crippling osteo-arthritis and rheumatoid arthritis which tormented her during the later years of her life. As she was allergic to traditional medicine, she sought relief from alternative sources, but despite being cared for by a devoted practitioner in homeopathy, she eventually lost the battle and passed away. An enormous loss to all of us.

Orchard Cottage is a place of warmth and comfort, a place which enfolds you with its peace – the place of inspiration for all my spiritual work. Memories pass through the mind as I write.

– The awesome silence and stillness of the cottage in deep snow.

– Large family occasions – Michael's parents' Golden Wedding Anniversary, his mother's 80th and 90th Birthday celebrations, gazebos on the lawn, a huge throng of guests each time, filling the cottage and garden with happy laughter.

– Sweltering summers – parched and yellowed lawns: would it ever rain again?

– Christmas – the cottage at its best – festive indoor lights, mulled wine around the fireside, a stack of logs, family and friends gathered together. And of course, the Tree.

– A place of rich heritage, golden memories, peace and tranquillity.

– Oak beams, latch doors, flagstones, log fires – cobwebs, endless cobwebs.

– Ants, wasps, hornets, deer ravaging the roses, bats flitting hither and thither at dusk, gigantic spiders, even peacocks wandering in from neighbouring gardens. All kinds of wild life – some welcome, some not so.

– Cottage tasks – polishing the brass and silver, shelling peas, chopping wood, cutting the beech hedge, always trying to tame a rampaging garden.

– Putting in the wooden staircase beautifully designed by Michael so that we could have easier access to the loft rooms than the previous ladder and trapdoor had allowed! Thus an extra bedroom en suite and improved office accommodation for Michael's architectural practice became available.

– Memories of good times and the not so good – and into this category has to come the Pear Tree Disaster! During a great storm our pear tree blew down across the front lawn, falling onto power cables attached to the chimney stack causing it to crash down through the roof, creating thousands of pounds worth of damage in an instant, with the resultant loss of power and frugal camping within for some considerable time after.

I am constantly amazed by nature's ability to repair and renew itself so that the restoration has resulted in an even more beautiful environment than before.

Orchard Cottage has indeed served as a place of sanctuary for the greater part of our married life.

\* \* \*

*View from an Orchard Cottage window*

# SECTION VI

Significant Influences

Part I: Sixth Form Awakenings

Part II: Father Alan Cotgrove, Cowley Fathers

Part III: An Oxford Mystic

Part IV: Rev. Dr. Douglas Young
(his ministry and The Definitions)

Part V: Rt. Rev. John Dennis

Part VI: Very Rev. Alex Wedderspoon,
former Dean of Guildford – his retirement lecture:
A Faith for the 21st Century

Part VII: Intimations of Life After Death

Part VIII: The Fintry Community

# I

# SIXTH FORM AWAKENINGS

Most of us during teenage years or later go through a period when we question the deeper things of life, whether it be our political affiliation, our religious perspective, our values, allegiances or moral stance.

And when in the Sixth Form of our local High School, I was approached by a fellow student who took me aside and proceeded to indoctrinate me about the importance of 'becoming a Christian' as she put it. There followed a number of similar sessions during which she drew me closer and closer towards the conviction that such a commitment was right for me. Indeed it seemed to meet an unspoken need harboured for some years – and so it was that I embarked on my Christian journey.

I was rapidly swept up into the full 'evangelical' routine at the very time when Billy Graham was in Great Britain, 'leading people to Christ' at Haringey and other arenas around the country. Reading 'Daily Bread' issued by the Scripture Union together with Youth For Christ rallies, Bible study sessions and regular, committed church-going, all of this became part of my new routine. Everything else was excluded or rather, disapproved of: no 'normal' social life that other young people around me were enjoying, no cinemas or magazines, no bars or pubs on the grounds that 'living for Jesus' was enough and nothing more was necessary!

But, some years later, I started 'back-sliding' – sin of sins! I stopped going to church! I no longer felt at ease with this negative, restrictive, approach to life that such a strict routine had created deep within. Surely there was more to life than such a shallow approach? I wrestled with guilt, confusion and a sense of sin for some considerable time, resulting in a virtual spiritual breakdown!

# II

## FATHER ALAN COTGROVE, COWLEY FATHERS

Mercifully, my guilt and confusion were short-lived and fortuitously some years later, when career developments had taken me to Oxford, I happened to meet a member of the Cowley Fathers, Father Alan Cotgrove who virtually saved my life, or rather, saved my spiritual life from total disintegration.

It happened one afternoon while I was watching a table tennis match in a sports hall hired from the nearby Cowley Fathers. At one point in the match, a side door opened and in walked a black-robed figure who, to my consternation, was making his way up the side of the hall to where I was sitting on the only bench! I shuddered inside: 'I'm NOT going to get involved in a conversation with him,' I vowed. 'He will only talk about religion...' This was very much a taboo subject for me at that time. But sure enough, he came and sat beside me, at which point I rudely turned my back on him! This didn't put Father Alan Cotgrove off though, and very subtly, with quiet determination, he began winkling my spiritual 'state' out of me. I gradually relaxed and found myself talking freely, and with enormous relief, because at last I had found a truly compatible listener!

Through subtle but gentle probing, he soon realised I was in a hugely confused spiritual state and recognised that I was currently experiencing major doubts of faith and belief exactly as he himself had done many years earlier.

Mercifully, throughout the course of several subsequent meetings in the Chapel of the Cowley Fathers, he was able to completely re-inform my belief system, convincing me that spirituality – true spirituality – could be far wider, deeper, broader than anything I had experienced up to now, that we as human beings were on a spiritual journey, leading to true fulfilment. Our aim should be the very best that we could be – living life to the full – with a deep conviction and assurance, underpinning everything we do.

Thus it was with a lighter heart and total conviction that he and I parted – whereupon I discarded my stocks of Daily Bread and, uplifted by a newly invigorated prayer life, began living again.

# III

## AN OXFORD MYSTIC

While still in Oxford in the 1960s, working at the Radcliffe Infirmary, we had need of locum staff one summer, and into my office and into my life, arrived someone whom I can only describe as bombastic, boisterous and totally unlike anyone I had met before. But Honey, a middle aged mature woman, was immensely able. She had a brain like a razor, a voice like thunder which I resisted for as long as I could, until one day, she and I were alone whereupon her voice became less strident, much quieter and she embarked on a discourse about belief and spirituality which truly had me spellbound. I recognised immediately a voice of rare authority. Here indeed was someone who had a spiritual vision and awareness unlike any other – she was indeed, a true mystic. And with her deep perception and far reaching spiritual eye, my own belief system was now firmly cemented and I was ready to follow that golden string ever further.

\* \* \*

# IV

# REV. DR. DOUGLAS YOUNG

In the late 1960s, further career development led me eventually to London, to an administrative post at the Royal College of Surgeons where I organised medical conferences up and down the country.

During that period of some ten years or so, I enrolled for a course of lectures in Philosophy led by a gifted academic teacher, preacher and writer, Rev. Dr. Douglas Young.

He was yet to publish three books, all outlining the principles of philosophy, his intention always to express difficult concepts as clearly and simply as possible. 'Less is more' was his mantra.

During his lectures we invited him to define various words as below:

---

BRAIN: Is the physical instrument of the soul. The integrating factor of the entire body.

CONSCIENCE: Is the directly intuited word of God. As it often runs counter to habit, custom, education and reason, it cannot be attributed to these sources. It has to be listened out for. It is always costly to follow.

DEATH: Death is the transition from this life to the next. The grain of wheat 'dies' in order to progress to the plant. The present person 'dies' in order to become the more advanced being.

In the next stage of existence, we are recognisable but not by physical characteristics.

A good analogy of death is the transition of the earthbound grub into the airborne moth or butterfly. It achieves a new kind of body to enable it to move in a new medium. It gains 'a celestial' body as Paul puts it in I Corinthians.

EGO: Is almost to be equated with self, except that it has the overtones of 'willing' and 'deciding' and 'wanting' so – 'to satisfy one's ego.'

EMOTION: Strong feelings; emotion is the bridge between knowing and doing.

ETERNITY: Is continued time – never-ending time. It is to be distinguished from the word 'eternal' which in St. John's use, refers to a quality (rather than a quantity) of living. 'Now is eternal life' says John.

EVIL: Is anything contrary to the will of God. It is to be distinguished from sin which is conscious, wilful indulgence of evil. Hence one is responsible for sin but not necessarily for evil.

FAITH: Non-rational – though not irrational – trust in God. Believing where we cannot prove.

FEELING: Broad term which covers faint, undefined emotions as well as tactile sensory impressions.

GOD: Is the name we give to the ultimate creative Being. Because He is the creator of personal beings, He must Himself be at least personal. Jesus gave a picture of Him as a 'Heavenly Father' and tested the adequacy of all possible attributes by reference to this concept of the Fatherhood of God.

GOOD: Is that which is in accord with the will of God as revealed to us by Jesus.

HELL: A place of punishment usually held to be in the after-life. The Old Testament has many different concepts of Hell – ranging from annihilation to Sheol – a pit containing a gradation of punishments.

INSTINCT: Automatic reaction to a given stimulus. It is always common to a species.

INTELLECT: The activity of the brain involved in acts of judgment and cognition

INTUITION: Immediate (i.e. non-mediated) knowledge. For example, I intuit that I exist. 'Cogito ergo sum' though designed to reduce the immediacy of the knowledge of self to the mediation of thought begs the question, 'what mediates the knowledge of your thoughts?'

LIFE: Can mean many things:

(a) Anything which by its nature, moves. Today, this means ALL things, for all things – even stones – have internal movement.

(b) That which characterizes organic matter – say a kitten as distinct from a piece of wood.

(c) That which is characterized by identity and resistance to environment. That is, 'real living' is denoted by the possession of an ideal and the power to resist environmental distractions so that the ideal becomes possessed and reached.

MAN: Is a creature of God. He has evolved through various lower stages of life and thus has pulls and inner urges in two directions – downward to a previous ancestry characterised by animal wants and upward to an ideal state exemplified by Jesus, the archetype of man as he should be and could be.

MIND: Is the totality of one's thoughts.

PERSONALITY: In a broader sense, those features which distinguish a person from, say, a stone. In another sense, that individuation, which distinguishes one person from another. To an existentialist, it is these distinguishing individuating factors which alone are real and worthwhile.

PRAYER: The means of communication between man and God. Also, just coming into God's company consciously and with purpose: putting oneself in the state of mind in which one is suggestible to God's word.

REASON: The act of reaching a conclusion by putting together non-linked data. It can be a priori (i.e. reached AHEAD of experience or obtained by hindsight.)

RIGHT: Is that which concurs with a standard. It need not refer to that which is intrinsically good.

SELF: Is the essential personality, plus all the 'accidens' which individuate.

SOUL: Is the total, individual personality.

THOUGHT: A non-expressed judgment.

SPIRIT: Is that part or activity of the soul which makes contact with God.

WILL: Is the act of decision, the putting into motion of one's wishes. It is NOT to be equated with the strongest wish.

WRONG: That which offends against a standard. It need not refer to an intrinsic wrong.

---

His teaching and preaching had a profound effect on my life at an important time of spiritual growth.

He and his wife, Muriel, became very dear friends while I was in London and although Douglas died some years ago, Michael and I still keep in touch with Muriel, now in Yorkshire, within easy reach of her family.

\* \* \*

# V

# RT. REV. JOHN DENNIS

I had the immense good fortune to meet with this inspiring figure some years later while in Guildford, setting up my first major spiritual project Cultural Country Retreats.

During my initial approach to the Anglican Bishops in this country for support and backing prior to the launch of CCR, John Dennis, then Bishop of St. Edmundsbury and Ipswich, was one of the most supportive, and was behind me throughout the duration of the concept. 'It is of God' he used to say. He became Chairman of our Advisory Board, lending wisdom and perception to our deliberations.

He also contributed to my first book, 'Five Gold Rings', and I give below an extract from his writing in which he selected the Person who had had the greatest impact on his life:

---

Canon Holder – a gentle, loving, elderly man who, certainly filled my mind for the first time with the intellectual realities of the Christian faith but who even more significantly, filled my heart with a burning desire to be like him. He was, for me, the incarnation of what Christian faith and love and hope and joy looked like. By the end of his confirmation classes, not only was I convinced of the reality of the Christian faith, I was also convinced that I was being called to the priesthood.

---

He retired to Winchester in 1996 and these days, he serves as my spiritual director – his wise counsel keeping me 'afloat' on my developing spiritual journey.

\* \* \*

# VI

# THE VERY REV. ALEX WEDDERSPOON

Alex Wedderspoon served as Dean of Guildford from 1987 to 2001 and Michael and I counted ourselves most fortunate to be in Guildford during this time.

He was much loved by all whose lives he touched: dignified, scholarly, a brilliant and gifted preacher, a sensitive pastor with a dry, pervasive sense of humour.

Although reluctant to leave Winchester, Alex was soon at home in Guildford. The cathedral's austere white interior suited his style. Worship and preaching of the highest standard was his aim and, while always ready to delegate responsibility to colleagues and provide them with strong support, he kept his finger on the pulse of every part of the cathedral's life.

Some of his finest sermons were published as 'A City set on a Hill' in 2001, in which Susan Howatch wrote in her Foreword:

---

*In 1987 during a period of difficulty in my personal life I decided to go to Guildford Cathedral to hear the Dean preach. I was not a regular churchgoer then and I knew nothing about Alex Wedderspoon except that he had only recently arrived in Guildford but although I entered the Cathedral in despair I emerged transformed. The sermon had given me not only the strength 'to keep on keeping on' as the Dean himself put it, but the conviction that all would eventually be well. That sermon on St. Paul's Epistle to the Romans, Chapter Eight, verse twenty-eight, appears in this book of his sermons and years after I heard it, I made the Dean's exposition of this text a central motif in the last of my series of novels about the Church of England.*

*Sermons matter. Alex Wedderspoon grapples with all the key issues of life, and in looking at them through his powerful Christian lens, we find they lose their ability to diminish us.*

Alex Wedderspoon was indeed a clergyman who practised what he preached and his exceptional sermons bear witness both to his distinguished ministry and his outstanding gifts.

This book, 'A City Set on a Hill', which Alex wrote 'represents the attempt of an ordinary working clergyman to talk some kind of sense to an intelligent congregation in the context of the difficulties, confusion and uncertainties of the closing years of the 20th century.'

It contains a wealth of spiritual insights:

Jesus, by his life, teaching, death and resurrection saves us from:

>   A Life without Meaning
>   A Life without Values
>   A Life without Hope

And in a sermon on 'Growing Older', he wrote:

>   ...those with
>   A Purpose to live for
>   A Self to Live with
>   A Faith to Live by

are indeed likely to live more happily in their senior years – a decline perhaps of their physical power but these people had gone on growing in the things of the spirit – courage – faith – hope – love – humour – patience and kindliness – for it is the things which are seen that are temporal but the things which are not seen, are eternal.

Upon his retirement as Dean of Guildford, Alex Wedderspoon gave a lecture to the Guildford Cathedral Community, entitled 'A Faith for the 21st Century' – some notes of which (believed to be his own) are attached.

And this surely speaks for itself of Alex's academic prowess and his far reaching spiritual vision.

* * *

# A FAITH FOR THE 21ST CENTURY

Very Rev. Alex Wedderspoon, Dean Of Guildford,
Wednesday 27th June 2001, Cathedral Education Centre:
(Some brief notes attributed to him)

Our Christian faith is, today, a religion in crisis.

We don't look to the fourth century for our medicine – so why therefore do we do so for our religion? If we compare the London of 2001 with the London of centuries ago, we see huge changes in architecture etc. St. Paul's for instance, is dwarfed by the surrounding new buildings.

An enormous revolution in thought over the last 50 years – huge revolution in science, technology etc. In parallel to this is the revolution in behavioural sciences. Sociologists today dismiss religion as out of date and as something invented by man. A huge revolution in our attitude to the authority of the Bible. For centuries the Bible was thought of as the word of God – now only considered as religious literature and subject to question along with everything else. Religious belief has also been swept away over recent years – radical beliefs have been questioned and explained away. Religion is merely a word for the highest personal ideals. That's all it is – They say.

These kind of statements attract huge publicity today. Whereas in previous centuries, faith was criticised only behind closed doors in monasteries, now it is wide open to criticism from all sides – for instance on television.

The person of Jesus Christ is seen as anything from the incarnation of God to a spirit-inspired prophet. Critics go through the synoptic gospels and discard much of it. There is a tremendous awareness of other world religions – all are seen as good in their own right – all are valid belief systems. Also we have the catastrophic influence of two major world wars – which brings people to ask: how does God allow this? How can a God of love allow this?

Tremendous influence of popular culture. Huge revolution of sexual morality in the 50s and 60s. The emancipation of women – the church seen as a highly diverse belief system. In our western world enormous improvements in our affluence and quality of life. People no longer yearn for the after-life as an escape from this one – they are more than happy here.

Thus a steady withdrawal from religious practice. It's as though religious belief is seen as a bombed city from the air – nothing much left.

Now less than 9% of our country has some kind of church contact and by the year 2020, it is estimated that there will be no members of the Church of Scotland.

Despite this, there is today a huge interest in spirituality. An extraordinary outburst of moving and expressive spirituality for instance at Princess Diana's funeral which mystified many. Strong evangelical churches are flourishing. House groups are growing.

So what should be our approach to a faith for the 21st century?

'My face shall not be seen…' (i.e. the hidden ness of God), is affirmed by all religions. He cannot be proved by intellectual argument. The ultimate, sacred mystery. The source. The light. Cosmic reality and profound mystery.

To understand God – in line with very limited awareness – it is as though we are locked in a cage with only five slits to see out. Can only see a very tiny part of a whole.

Each one of us is a cell of energy living in this vast whole cell of energy. One way of picturing this is by considering the rest of the human body. Mystics see this of great importance. Many see it this way (i.e. that we are cells in the cosmic body of God) – the totality of the cosmos. Our mind and spiritual mind connects with God and we are co-creators in that mystery. Bede Griffiths wrote of this: 'we are all one'.

Men and women are spiritual beings having a human experience: they are not human beings having a spiritual experience.

We receive insights from all the other religions. There is evidence of order, beauty, reality, of love and goodness, of the reality of mystical experience.

A person's approach to this depends on their place of birth (i.e. Anglican, Jew etc.)

We need to see God in the total pluralistic setting. We live our earthly lives on a need-to-know basis but this cannot apply to our spiritual lives.

Who is Jesus? Who was Jesus? What can we now believe? Birth stories are now seen as legends – the whole emphasis later on is on the humanity of Jesus. A man approved of God. A man with a unique inner consciousness of God. A man of holiness. The coming of the Kingdom of God – not a vast cosmic event – we should ignore apocalyptic prophesies – remove all references to the coming of the Kingdom as a vast event.

Jesus was a Healer and exorcist. A teacher, a prophet, a man of God. A man of the spirit. Inspired by the spirit – manifesting unseen energy coming from the Divine. Was fully human. Had inner doubts and questionings. This is a more real interpretation than that seen on a stained glass window. Jesus in his teaching was not a theologian. Emphasized certain things basic to the life of the spirit. (see 'A Perennial Philosophy' by Aldus Huxley).

In his teaching, Jesus referred to certain key points regarding the life of the spirit.

- *The Kingdom of God is within you. Inner divinity.*

- *When we speak of God, we refer to a Being of compassion and mercy, a Father*

- *God of grace (i.e. reality is gracious. We do not need to live in fear.)*

- *We relate to God directly (i.e. through the prayer of the publican)*

- *The care of the life of the Spirit – from the inner life, all else comes.*

- *The essential centrality of faith and trust. This faith and trust nourishes hope.*

- *The mind and heart of love is compassion – for oneself and all humanity.*

Jesus emphasized certain themes for the health of our spiritual life:

- *The preservation of an attitude of awe and wonder*

- *The central place of an attitude of gratitude*

- *Spiritual awareness: blessed are those who are aware of their need of God.*

- *Openness to the shadow side of our existence; having compassion towards grief and sorrow.*

- *Concern for right and responsible living*

- *Concern for ideals of personal integrity*

- *The nurture of a forgiving and merciful spirit: 'you must forgive yourself' (i.e. profound compassion for ourselves).*

- *Avoidance of over-anxiety for things of this world.*

In earlier times, there were no codes laid down for human sexual behaviour – women for instance were no more than chattels for men. If a woman could not conceive, it was considered to be the will of God. Today she would be sent to a Fertility Clinic. The whole culture of sexual morality of the Old Testament and New Testament is light years away from where we are today.

Jesus took for granted life eternal, a large part of the Gospels devoted to the Passion narrative – demonstrates the triumph of love over death.

The nature of life eternal is often discussed today – the idea of our continuing spiritual development in a higher state plus the idea of reincarnation. Much argument about this – is it a reality or just chemistry of the brain?

For example, the blind born people who have had near-death experiences – can recall visually what they saw in a near death experience although they were born blind and have never seen these things in real life. Also hypnotic regression – refer to previous lives and life of the spirit. All these things are worthy of thought.

In conclusion, given the huge gulf between the religion of Jesus and the religion about Jesus as it has been elaborated by churches – where are we and where do we go?

The Church today is the subject of profound change. An enormous growth today of the church in Africa – yet huge decline in the Western world.

Religious groups will continue as long as they make no claim to arrogance and certainty. They will preserve and study the teachings. They will provide the Offices of marriages, baptism etc. Voluntary euthanasia will come. Hospices of light. Ministries of healing will continue. Churches will continue but will be vastly different.

Jesus emphasized the essential place of the spiritual life which is 'within you.' Jesus taught the reality of the Secret Place, the inner room. Intense inner reality of the private chapel of their minds – those in solitary confinement have found this. The place of inner stillness. Jesus taught us the Lord's Prayer and the whole of later Christian tradition stresses the importance of some pattern of private prayer.

- *We live within unconditional love.*

- *Importance of retreats – times of withdrawal, times of solitude, times of rest.*

- *What drains the spirit, drains the body.*

- *The importance of a Rule of Rest, a Rule of Prayer, a Rule of Work.*

- *Spiritual life is also about coming alive.*

- *The reality of divine experience through living in the spirit.*

- *No division between the sacred and secular. Should include living to the full (i.e. Friendship. Literature. Celebrations and Festivals. Being Real, Human and Alive.)*

- *Theosis: realisation of our inner divinity. Whole cosmos seems to be about this inner growth and transformation.*

This might be a way in which we could be seeing a faith which bears some relationship to truth and can carry us forward into the 21st century. It is important that we should not feel threatened by the changes endemic in society.

**p.p. AW**
**June 2001**

# VII

## INTIMATIONS OF LIFE AFTER DEATH

In writing of the various significant influences on my life, I feel compelled to include an account of a meaningful encounter with a gifted medium with whom I was in touch, through a friend in Guildford, some years after losing my mother.

I wrote the attached article 'A personal experience of survival after death' for the Journal of The Churches' Fellowship for Psychical and Spiritual Studies and reproduced it here with kind permission of the Editor.

There are some who feel that with a deep Christian faith, there is no need to 'supplement' such a conviction with forays into this 'otherness' of life – indeed it might be frowned upon so to do – but there is a school of thought within the Christian faith – hence the establishment of the highly reputable Churches' Fellowship for Psychical and Spiritual Studies – that lends credence to the relevance of such exploration in support of Christian belief. Such exploration within a 'safe' environment, has been the source of comfort and reassurance to many.

Another significant and encouraging influence on my life.

\* \* \*

# A PERSONAL EXPERIENCE OF SURVIVAL AFTER DEATH

My parents' marriage had been a deeply unhappy relationship and their incompatibility eventually drove my mother into a regime of alcohol and sleeping pills – the only form of escape she knew. Her life of deep unhappiness was tragically and suddenly cut short by choking to death in a restaurant with my father.

Apart from the shock of her sudden death, I was disturbed by the fact that she had died in such an unhappy frame of mind – I feared she might become a 'lost' or 'restless' soul – unable to find the peace which she had so desperately craved on earth.

During an unexpected opportunity for a sitting with a renowned Medium some 12 months later, I explained the unhappy circumstances of my mother's death to the Medium and asked if he could 'get through' to her so that I might be reassured that all was well. To my joy, he immediately made contact and it became clear that my mother was happily reunited with former friends and family, naming several by their nicknames – proof to me this was no hoax. The Medium transcribed further words from my mother, to say how much she had loved the cross-shaped wreath of white lilies we had made for her funeral – how much she approved of my (then) new husband – 'but tell him not to work so hard' – how she loved our cottage with roses everywhere... The Medium stopped at this point and spoke to me.

'Your mother is now describing a wooden box this big,' and he spread his hands to indicate its size, 'with a carved edging to the lid and a painting of flowers on the top. Does this mean anything to you because your mother would like you to have it.'

My heart leapt – he was describing a wooden box my mother used to keep her artwork in for making Barbola – a special kind of jewellery which could be painted and varnished. My mother had been very artistic and I knew the box well from childhood but as my parents had moved house so many times, I had no idea where the box was now – or even if it had survived the various moves. Because of her sudden death, she had not made a will – so there had been no personal items bequeathed either to me or my sister.

The session with the Medium closed. Later, I described its outcome to my husband.

'That box is upstairs in our attic,' he declared. 'I retrieved it from your father's garage after he died and thought it might be valuable but forgot to tell you!'

He brought it down – and to my amazement – it was indeed The Box and I knew then beyond all doubt that my mother had survived death and was now reunited with her loved ones. And wanted me to know.

**AJ**
**Nov 06**

# VIII

# THE FINTRY COMMUNITY

This latest of significant influences on my life has been through The Fintry Community at Brook, Nr.Milford, Surrey.

Fintry is home to The Fintry Trust and the Universal Order, both of which are dedicated to the teaching of the Universal ideas and ideals which underlie all traditions.

An arts and crafts house with extensive and impressive grounds, it serves as both a retreat house and a venue for events, covering the arts, science, religion and mysticism. It is run by a Trust and a small dedicated group of volunteers and maintains its identity as a haven of peace.

Many people experience an indefinite spiritual longing for something beyond their current circumstances, something purer and more lasting. Others feel themselves alone in upholding principles not obviously valued by society. Established religion may not always help, yet neither do passing fashions and schools of thought fully satisfy this need.

I have been richly blessed through an enduring friendship with a senior member of this Order and have benefited hugely from discussions with her on matters of deep spiritual significance. Indeed, she is a powerhouse of spiritual perception, mystical insights, and her gentle presence continues to uplift, encourage and inspire, whenever we meet. It is a privilege to be blessed with such a friendship.

\* \* \*

# The Fintry Trust

**Fintry**
**Brook**
**Godalming**
**Surrey GU8 5UQ**
**UK**

*www.thefintrytrust.org.uk*

Educational Charity Reg. No.313286

*Anna: Looking to the future...*

# SECTION VII

Highdays & Holidays

# HIGHDAYS & HOLIDAYS

From these earlier reflections on my spiritual journey, it should not be assumed that I spend all my days on my knees with a prayer mat out 24/7! Vital though prayer is, it is also essential that we balance our lives - with Being and Doing so that essential breaks are programmed into our routine, giving adequate opportunities for rest and relaxation.

Holidays and travel have featured prominently for me as an essential component of this balance, both prior to and since marriage.

Thus it was that my first experience of flying came early in my twenties, when I had an opportunity to explore Yugoslavia (now Serbia and Croatia) with a girlfriend. We were based in Ljubljana – a place of ice blue seas, sun and sand – and those two weeks were totally exhilarating. I loved every minute.

Some years later, while living in London, I travelled much further afield – to the USA, spending three weeks with Douglas and Muriel Young, friends who were based in Boston, New England, undertaking a pulpit exchange. My time with them came during The Fall, with New England at its glorious best. Apart from experiencing for the first time the culture and scenic differences, I had an opportunity to join the local community to celebrate Thanksgiving, the memories of which are still as vibrant as ever. A long drive into the hills led to a cabin style house where a long, long table seating 20 to 30, had been set, stretching the length of the ground floor; it was spread lavishly with pies of every size and description, as was the custom at Thanksgiving, accompanied by happy chatter, wine flowing, the first snow falling.

Later during that time in Boston, I came across this poster:

> *We are born alone, we die alone –*
> *this time called life was meant to share*

A meaningful, must-have memento of my time there.

Early in my marriage to Michael, I travelled to Germany for a very special and significant performance of the Oberammergau Passion Play in 1984. The play is normally performed every ten years but on this occasion it was held to mark its 350th anniversary. And today, if I listen hard, I can still hear the tramp of feet as the audience, coming from every direction, walked through the streets of Oberammergau to converge on the theatre at the village centre. An all-day performance with a long lunch break, as is the custom. It was one of the most memorable experiences of my life.

Some years later, Michael and I returned to Europe. He was now a member of the Vivace Chorus, and as such, we participated in a choral tour of France including sublime choral performances in three cathedrals – Rouen, Beauvais and Notre Dame, Paris.

A visit to Germany followed soon after while staying with friends near Munich, from where we explored the spectacular delights of Bavaria and nearby Salzburg.

And then, later on, to Europe yet again, with the Guildford-Freiburg Association, to their base in Freiburg with all the delights of that city to explore; the Freiburg Munster, hill-top restaurants, the morning market in streets surrounding the cathedral, gigantic displays of fruit, vegetables, buckets of glorious flowers, wood carvings, sweets and other delicacies, a tempting array of gifts to take home from that vast display.

But not only did these overseas adventures offer essential relaxation, but country walking, which has always been an essential part of our holiday planning. Favourite areas include the Lake District, Pembrokeshire, Cornwall, The Cotswolds, Isle of Wight, Dorset, South Downs, Surrey – all offering a unique piece of paradise.

Michael and I have found walking to be an immensely enjoyable form of relaxation with inspirational scenery, compatible company – wining and dining at the end of the day – why would anyone crave the beaches of Spain when the countryside is free for the taking – or rather the walking? In the wide open space of the countryside, with the feel of turf under feet, 'our souls could quieten and then expand' as another walker friend put it so beautifully. And R.S. Thomas writes movingly in his masterpiece

*The Moor:*

*It was like a church to me,*
*I entered it on soft foot,*
*Breath held like a cap in the hand,*
*It was quiet.*
*What God was there made himself felt,*
*Not listened to, in clean colours*

*That brought a moistening of the eye,*
*In movement of the wind over grass.*

*There were no prayers said. But stillness*
*of the heart's passions – that was praise*
*Enough; and the mind's cession*
*Of its kingdom. I walked on,*
*Simple and poor, while the air crumbled*
*And broke on me generously as bread*

Believing as I do that we are spiritual beings on a human journey, we need therefore to balance the pressures of life with essential refreshment - country walking certainly offers that.

*Anna on holiday in Corfe Castle, with Michael*

# SECTION VIII

Earning a Crust!

# EARNING A CRUST

Extreme good fortune has been a major factor throughout my working life, and I have been blessed with amazing opportunities that have opened up before me. While not wishing to itemize all the minutiae of my Curriculum Vitae, nevertheless three posts in particular stand out as probably the most fulfilling and rewarding of my working life.

The first, during the ten years I was living in St. John's Wood, London, I landed an administrative role at the Royal College of Surgeons, a prestigious building in Lincoln's Inn Fields. This post involved heading a Secretariat which looked after the administrative affairs of two specialist Associations – the British Association of Physical Medicine and the Association of Anaesthetists for Great Britain and Ireland. The Officers of both of these were full-time consultants at nearby London Hospitals and while they directed the affairs of the Association under the instruction of their Councils, all the follow-up and basic administration was passed to the Secretariat – meaning I worked with the minimum of supervision, organising annual dinners, council meetings, correspondence, financial affairs and all the associated administration involved with the position. The post involved travel up and down the country and I loved every minute.

However, the pittance that was my salary eventually forced me to seek a more lucrative post with a similar Association, this time focussed on education – the Association of Colleges for Further and Higher Education. This again meant working on my own, running the London Office with an Honorary Secretary who was then Principal of a Cambridge College. My work involved all the administration of a professional Association – the organisation of and travel to their conferences up and down the country, finance, daily correspondence, attendance at meetings and all the other supportive work needed to keep a professional Association afloat, so to speak.

These two posts occupied me for the ten years I was in London until marriage eventually took me to Guildford.

But before that – let me recount an extraordinarily moving experience I had while on a London bus one Saturday morning.

## On a London Bus

It was a habit of mine to travel into central London most Saturday mornings for some retail therapy and on this particular day, I boarded the 159 taking me down Lisson Grove towards Baker Street. The morning was bright, the bus not particularly full and my thoughts were idling as they do while travelling. I was not depressed or particularly concerned about anything at all.

We stopped at the traffic lights just before Baker Street and then, quietly, without warning, time seemed to stand still for what must have been moments but seemed like a lifetime. I was transported into a space of essential stillness, as if to another dimension and was aware of being enveloped in an outpouring of calm; the immediacy of things receded, almost faded and I had the strongest sense of being reassured from a source beyond that all would be well, not only on a personal level but also globally. A sense of almost tangible peace completely overwhelmed me - indeed, such a transcendental experience was something I shall never forget. Words never seem able to do justice to it.

*** 

A year or so later, another interesting and somewhat fortuitous experience occurred just before moving to Guildford while travelling on the London underground. I picked up an abandoned free paper, and discovered a feature on careers, describing the work of an Administrator of a Postgraduate Medical Education Centre. It appealed immensely but at that time, there was simply no clear route to such a coveted post!

However, a few years later, in Guildford, I was offered a supportive role in the Postgraduate Medical Centre of the local hospital, and later, a promotional opportunity led to my being appointed their Administrator, thus I had secured that very same coveted role that I had read about in London while on the underground a few years earlier! Was this a strange coincidence or part of a life-plan? Whichever, for the next ten years, it proved to be one of the happiest periods in my working life, bringing me into contact with a wide range of hospital staff at all levels: pharmaceutical companies, an impressive team of medical and surgical staff serving as Tutors, General Practitioners, Dental staff, para-medical staff, and my own team of loyal helpers without whom I could not have survived! Latterly while the new Postgraduate Centre was being built on the other side of town, I found myself running two centres – one either side of Guildford. This was not just a job but a vocation and long, long hours were involved which I gave without hesitation.

One of the greatest thrills of my working life occurred just prior to the opening of Phase I of the new Royal Surrey County Hospital where a temporary post-graduate medical education centre had been established. HM the Queen had accepted an invitation to open the new hospital and as Administrator of the Centre, I was nominated to represent it along with other Departmental Heads – and to my utter amazement, I had the opportunity to meet and speak with Her Majesty! Astonished by how tiny she is, gifted with that unique ability to focus 100% on each person she meets – it was a truly unforgettable experience.

But eventually, Michael found himself having to question my devotion to the hospital with the comment: 'Are you married to me or the Medical Centre dear?'

Brought to the brink of shame because of my divided loyalties, I sought alternative employment – to preserve my marriage!

\* \* \*

# SECTION IX

Rounding Off...

# ROUNDING OFF...

In this closing section, first a moment to return to the starting point – to the Twinship which has bound Judy and myself together from that moment of birth. And to the inescapable closeness we have shared from the womb – as two halves rather than a biological whole. Has this made each of us less of a person than had we been one? I often muse on this. However, both of us have chosen our separate life paths, as decreed by circumstance.

Believing as I do in karmic choices and the consequence of former lives, I am convinced Judy and I have chosen to be reincarnated as a twin, both of us needing to work through our purpose for being here. Doubtless we have different lessons to learn, for different reasons. She, for instance, may well be here to help me learn understanding and patience, as indeed I could be here to help her grow spiritually and see life's challenges as opportunities.

There was a time, upon marriage, that loyalty to Edward, her husband took natural priority over the twinship and we drew apart for a while – thus I was forced to redefine my own life, 'twinless' as it were. But upon her husband's sudden death twelve years ago, she has needed to retrieve the original closeness that we enjoyed in childhood – the total giving and sharing that marks a twin. This need has greatly challenged my own marriage and indeed, Michael's tolerance and understanding.

But the twinship has, nevertheless survived, as has my own marriage, because of the unique bonds contained within each relationship – needing maturity and tolerance from all of us. As someone famous was heard to say, 'There are three of us in this marriage!'

And so we come back again to karma and to the choices we have made in order to learn the karmic lessons as we perceive them.

*** 

But something rather extraordinary is worth a mention here. Recently I was turning out papers at home and came across some notes I made after an encounter with a medium many, many years ago. This medium had predicted that 'the spiritual side of my life would be outstanding and that when I looked back, I would be amazed. This work would not be due to my own efforts but to the Spirit Force working through me. I would be merely an instrument.'

I **am** amazed – it is quite an astonishing discovery – reading these notes years later. Notes which have lain in a drawer for some forty years, totally forgotten. Yet I find it strangely moving and humbling that my spiritual life has indeed developed in ways I could never have imagined – that golden string has truly been leading me along a path foretold for me all those years ago.

*** * ***

So now, what of the future, as I contemplate what may lie ahead? Firstly – an ongoing prayer:

*Lord, give me health until my work is done*
*and work until my life is done.*

And then deep gratitude to all who have featured so magnificently in the high spots of my life as well as those who have held my hand through the darker, more challenging times. Gratitude also to my twin for giving me the opportunity to learn the karmic lessons referred to above.

I cannot help but wonder how much more winding of that golden thread there may be for me, but whether a short length or longer, I am consoled by the anonymous words of 'Tapestry of My Life', Rudyard Kipling's wonderfully humorous poem 'When Earth's Last Picture is Painted' and lastly by the immortal words of Mother Julian of Norwich:

> All shall be well
> And all shall be well
> And all manner of things shall be well

*** * ***

**Anna Jeffery**
**Autumn 2016**
**Guildford**

# SECTION X

Afterwords...

# Tapestry of My Life

I wonder what the other side will be when I have finished weaving all my thread. I do not know the pattern nor the end of this great piece of work which is for me. I only know that I must weave with care the colors that are given me, day by day, and make of them a fabric firm and true, which will be of service for my fellow man. Sometimes those colors are so dark and gray I doubt if there will be one line or trace of beauty there. But all at once there comes a thread of gold or rose so deep that there will always be that one bright spot to cherish or to keep and maybe against its ground of darker hue it will be beautiful!

The warp is held in place by the Master's hand. The Master's mind made the design for me; if I but weave the shuttle to and fro and blend the colors just the best I know, perhaps when it is finished, He will say, "Tis good," and lay it on the footstool of His feet.

# TAPESTRY OF MY LIFE

I wonder what the other side will be when I have finished weaving all my thread. I do not know the pattern nor the end of this great piece of work which is for me. I only know that I must weave with care the colours that are given me, day by day, and make of them a fabric firm and true, which will be of service for my fellow man. Sometimes those colours are so dark and grey, I doubt if there will be one line or trace of beauty there. But all at once there comes a thread of gold or rose so deep that there will always be that one bright spot to cherish or to keep and maybe against its ground of darker hue it will be beautiful!

The warp is held in place by the Master's hand. The Master's mind made the design for me; if I but weave the shuttle to and fro and blend the colours just the best I know, perhaps when it is finished, He will say 'Tis good' and lay it on the footstool of His feet.

Anonymous

# WHEN EARTH'S LAST PICTURE IS PAINTED
## By Rudyard Kipling

When Earth's last picture is painted
    and the tubes are twisted and dried,
When the oldest colours have faded,
    and the youngest critic has died,
We shall rest, and, faith, we shall need it –
    lie down for an aeon or two,
Till the Master of All Good Workmen
    shall put us to work anew.

And those that were good shall be happy:
    they shall sit in a golden chair;
They shall splash at a ten-league canvas
    with brushes of comet's hair.
They shall find real saints to draw from –
    Magdalene, Peter and Paul;
They shall work for an age at a sitting
    and never be tired at all!

And only The Master shall praise us,
    and only The Master shall blame;
And no one shall work for money,
    and no one shall work for fame,
But each for the joy of the working,
    and each, in his separate star,
Shall draw the Thing as he sees it
    for the God of Things as They are!

\* \* \*

................... what I do is me: for that I came


**As Kingfishers Catch Fire**
Gerard Manley Hopkins

# ACKNOWLEDGEMENTS

I am particularly grateful to The Hamblin Trust for allowing me to reprint the five articles I have written for their journal – New Vision – as under:

**The Heart of the Matter**

First published in the Spring 2014 edition of New Vision, journal of the Hamblin Trust and reprinted by kind permission of the Editor

**Acceptance**

First published in the Winter 2014 edition of New Vision, journal of the Hamblin Trust and reprinted by kind permission of the Editor

**A Trilogy on Truth**

First published in the Spring 2015 edition of New Vision, journal of the Hamblin Trust and reprinted by kind permission of the Editor

**Essential Connections**

First published in the Winter 2015 edition of New Vision, journal of the Hamblin Trust and reprinted by kind permission of the Editor

**Held in perfect balance**

First published in the Summer 2016 edition of New Vision, journal of the Hamblin Trust and reprinted by kind permission of the Editor

I am also grateful to the Churches' Fellowship for Spiritual and Psychic Studies for allowing me to reprint an article I wrote for their Summer 2008 Quarterly Review: 'Intimations of Life after Death'

My thanks are also due to Mrs. Judith Wedderspoon for permission to reprint the notes made on her husband's pre-retirement lecture: 'A Faith for the 21st Century' by the Very Rev. Alex Wedderspoon, former Dean of Guildford Cathedral.

And also to Mrs. Bobbin Baxter for professional assistance given in the editing of this MS – and from whom – together with my husband Michael and my twin sister Judy – came their conviction that I should prepare this account of my faith journey.

And lastly but by no means least, deep gratitude to the publishing team at Spiderwize – Haylee, Helen, Camilla and others who have worked so hard to fine tune my efforts and without whose professional expertise, this book would not be in your hands now!

Every effort has been made to trace the copyright owners of extracts included in 'The Gift' – but we apologise for any errors which might have occurred and would be glad to hear from the copyright owners of these extracts so that due acknowledgement can be made in all future editions of 'The Gift'.

# INDEX

**B**

Barrington-Ward, Rt Rev Simon .................................................. 33

**C**

Cathedral Dream ........................................................................ 61
Cathedral of the Isles, Cumbrae ................................................. 85
Churches Fellowship for Psychic and Spiritual Studies ............. 111
Cotgrove, Father Alan (Cowley Fathers) ..................................... 97
Cultural Country Retreats ........................................................... 20

**D**

Dennis, Rt.Rev John .................................................................. 103

**F**

Fintry Community ..................................................................... 114
Five Gold Rings (book) ............................................................... 32
Freeman Fr Laurence ................................................................. 34

**H**

Harries Rt Rev Richard ............................................................... 42
Harry Edwards Healing Sanctuary .............................................. 89

**K**

Kipling, Rudyard, When Earth's Last picture is painted ............ 132

## L

Lewis Judith – her poetry ................................................. 11-16
Life After Death, Intimations of ................................................. 111

## M

Marshall Rt Rev Michael ................................................. 35

## N

New Vision articles
    Heart of the Matter ................................................. 67
    Acceptance ................................................. 70
    Trilogy on Truth ................................................. 72
    Essential Connections ................................................. 75
    Held in Perfect Balance ................................................. 78

## O

On a London bus ................................................. 123
Orchard Cottage ................................................. 92

## P

Palmer, Rev Canon Dr.Maureen
    Towards a New Morality ................................................. 46
    Polkinghorne Rev Dr.John ................................................. 37
    Portmeirion ................................................. 87

## Q

Queen, Her Majesty, meeting with ................................................. 124

## S

Spirituality, definition of .................................................. 6
St.Cuthman's Retreat House ............................................. 82
St.Columba's Retreat House ............................................. 84
St.George's House, Windsor Castle ................................... 44
Symphony of Life (book)................................................... 50

## T

Tapestry of My Life ......................................................... 131
Transcendental moment on a London bus....................... 123
Tulley Sir Mark ................................................................. 39

## W

Weatherill Rt Hon the Lord.............................................. 40
Wedderspoon, Very Rev Alex ......................................... 104
A Faith for the 21st Century........................................... 106
When Earth's Last picture is painted (Rudyard Kipling)............ 132
Words, Music, Stillness...................................................... 57

## Y

Young, Rev Dr Douglas .................................................. 99

\* \* \*